George Devine studied at the University of San Francisco and Marquette University, and has taught at the latter institution, later joining the faculty of Seton Hall University, where he is now Chairman and Associate Professor in the Department of Religious Studies.

Professor Devine has been involved in the liturgical renewal of the Catholic Church throughout the United States for over a decade, and especially during the key years of transition in the mid-1960s. He also has numerous literary works to his credit, including articles and reviews in *The New York Times, Commonweal, The National Catholic Reporter, Worship, Catholic Currents, Catholic Digest, The Advocate, Christian Art, U.S. Catholic* and *Jubilee.* Alba House also has published his book *Transformation in Christ* (1972) in addition to the volumes he edited for the College Theology Society from 1970 to 1973.

LITURGICAL RENEWAL

Also By the Author:

Our Living Liturgy. Chicago: Claretian Publications, 1966.

Why Read the Old Testament? Chicago: Claretian Publications, 1966.

To Be A Man (ed.) Englewood Cliffs, N.J.: Prentice-Hall, Inc., 1969.

Theology in Revolution (ed.) Staten Island, N.Y.: Alba House, 1970.

New Dimensions in Religious Experience (ed.) Staten Island, N.Y.: Alba House, 1971.

Transformation in Christ. Staten Island, N.Y.: Alba House, 1972.

That They May Live: Theological Reflections on the Quality of Life (ed.) Staten Island, N.Y.: Alba House, 1972.

Por Que Debemos Leer El Antiguo Testamento. Chicago: Claretian Publications, 1972. Tr. Miguel A. Fernandez.

A World More Human, A Church More Christian (ed.) Staten Island, N.Y.: Alba House, 1973.

LITURGICAL RENEWAL

AN AGONIZING REAPPRAISAL

by

George Devine

ALBA · HOUSE   NEW · YORK

SOCIETY OF ST. PAUL, 2187 VICTORY BLVD., STATEN ISLAND, NEW YORK 10314

Library of Congress Cataloging in Publication Data

Devine, George, 1941-
    Liturgical renewal: an agonizing reappraisal

    Includes bibliographical references.
      1. Liturgics—Catholic Church—History.
I. Title.
BX1970. D454   264'.02   73-12923
ISBN 0-8189-0281-7

Nihil Obstat:
Austin B. Vaughn, S.T.D.
Censor Librorum

Imprimatur:
James P. Mahoney, D.D.
Vicar General, Archdiocese of New York
August 27, 1973

The Nihil Obstat and Imprimatur
are a declaration that a book or pamphlet is considered
to be free from doctrinal or moral error. It is not implied that those
who have granted the Nihil Obstat and Imprimatur agree with the contents,
opinions or statements expressed.

Designed, printed and bound in the United States of America by the Fathers
and Brothers of the Society of St. Paul, 2187 Victory Boulevard,
Staten Island, New York 10314, as part of their
communications apostolate.

1 2 3 4 5 6 7 8 9 (Current Printing: first digit).

FOREWORD

FOR OVER A DECADE, I have been professionally involved in the liturgical renewal of the Roman Catholic Church in the United States. This has involved experiences and reflections arising from situations including Latin *Missa recitata* and *Missa cantata*, English *Betsingmesse*, "dialogue Mass", English "high Mass", the macaronic liturgies of the first days after implementation of the Council's decrees, massive liturgical celebrations on a grand scale, "home Masses", and myriad para-liturgies. While much of this experience has been related in some way to my studies and teaching in theology (and thus to Catholic colleges and universities), a good deal of it has been in parishes, both as a professional director of community worship and as a parishioner, and some of it has been in hospitals (military and civilian), parochial schools, and a number of special situations. This experience has enabled me to learn much of the life of the Church in America (specifically the New York-New Jersey, Chicago-Milwaukee and San Francisco metropolitan areas) during a time of transition and adaptation not only in liturgy but in many other aspects of Catholic faith and practice as well. This book will allow me to share the experience, both intellectually and theologically and also practically.

I should hasten to add that this book is not for the congregation which is manifestly "advanced" in its liturgical development, except perhaps as a matter of passing interest or a sign of a kindred spirit. But the congregation which can truly say that its problems with liturgy are "licked" would be rare indeed, from all that I have seen, heard and ex-

[v]

perienced. Consequently, the practical approach of the volume is directed to what might be called the "typical" liturgical situation, rather than situations which would be at all special (e.g., colleges, schools, national parishes, etc.), although many of the suggestions herein will be worthwhile for special situations as well as more conventional ones. Moreover, I am presuming liturgical talents and resources which are no better than what commonly prevails in the average parish, again with the implication that the liturgically blessed congregation would probably find my suggestions largely otiose.

Finally, I am not trying to cover *all* the bases. For example, references will be made herein to the celebration of two sacraments other than the eucharist, viz., penance and matrimony, but not to the four others, in that the three sacramental rites to be treated occur more often in a public liturgical celebration than does one other (i.e., anointing of the sick), or because the others already are celebrated within a eucharistic context that affords a good deal of revitalized liturgical expression and experience (e.g., holy orders, and sometimes the sacraments of initiation).[1]

It is hoped, then, that the pastor, liturgist or layman in a somewhat typical liturgical assembly in English-speaking Christendom, but more specifically Catholic America,[2] will find this book useful for an understanding and implementation of liturgical renewal which may have been tried for a decade or more, but which has thus far been elusive. To that end, this work is offered.

---

1. For a detailed discussion, theologically and to some extent liturgically, of baptism and confirmation, cf. Chapter 4 of my book **Transformation In Christ** (Staten Island, N.Y.: Alba House, 1972).
2. This may include, but need not be restricted to, the society John Cogley describes in a book by that name (New York: Dial Press, 1973).

ACKNOWLEDGMENTS

This volume is hardly the work of a single author. It has been formed by the experiences and encouragement of so many. Some of these, pioneers in the renewal of the Catholic liturgy in America and elsewhere, have by now earned historical prominence, and are mentioned herein in that context. But there are others—literally too many to list by name—who have afforded this redactor much experience and encouragement in the liturgical apostolate. In the writing of this book, each of them—even if unknowingly—has played a part.

There are, moreover, those whose encouragement has been both conscious and constant. The author has in mind especially his colleagues at Seton Hall University, particularly Rev. John F. Morley and Rev. Richard M. Nardone, Assistant Professors of Religious Studies. The friendly encouragement of Dr. William Smith has also been valuable. The manuscript's preparation was greatly facilitated by the work of Mrs. Margaret Chiang, Miss Laura A. Waage and Miss Ann Brady in the Department of Religious Studies, and by Mr. Michael E. Gubernat, Rev. Mr. John A. Quill and Rev. Mr. Pasquale Papalia, former students now at Immaculate Conception Seminary, Darlington, N.J. Another student whose assistance has been extraordinary is Mr. Ralph N. Villanova, Jr. Encouragement also came from the author's brother, Mr. Peter M. Devine. The physical appearance of the book is the fine work of the Brothers of the Society of St. Paul, in their publishing division, Alba House, as part of their communications apostolate. Finally, the author is most indebted to those closest to him throughout the completion of this work, his wife Joanne and son George.

New York City   —George Devine
2 April 1973

[vii]

CONTENTS

[ix]

music begun by Popes Pius X[1] and XI and being carried on today. Relationships between clergy and musicians; choir and congregation. Principles for the selection and execution of liturgical music. Numerous specific concrete references.

Various suggestions for particular reforms concerning principles and practices in the celebration of the Mass-liturgy, as designed to fit different needs and situations. Consideration of the home liturgy, the dialogue homily, use of contemporary readings and other specific questions.

Specific suggestions for a renewed celebration of Penance, with a treatment of the historical background and theological evidence involved. The question of individual confession and absolution as opposed to group confession and/or absolution. Pertinent notions regarding the nature of sin and reconciliation.

Common Catholic problems and misunderstandings concerning the celebration of Matrimony. Christian Marriage rediscovered as a "social sacrament". Problems of congregational involvement. New liturgical forms to express new theological and human insights into sexuality. Suggestions for renewed celebrations of the nuptial liturgy.

FOR
My Mother

LITURGICAL RENEWAL

CHAPTER ONE

The Road to Renewal
Apostolic Times to the Turn of the Century

"To live," said John Henry Cardinal Newman, "is to change!" Our experience well bears out that great theologian's axiom. We are in many ways different from the persons we were as children: we are taller, stronger, wiser. We have grown by way of change. Yet, of course, we have not changed *completely* or *essentially*, because we are basically the same people we were before, even though our lives have consisted of many changes—changes which make us more fully the people we are today. And, of course, these changes are never really over. Life will continue to be a series of changes—changes by which we become fuller, more mature persons, more readily prepared to adapt to the situations of life and more suitably adjusted to the times and places we will be in.

Now, we are all members of the Church, the Body of Christ.[2] And this Body can be likened to our own bodies in many ways. One way in which the similarity is most striking is that of *change*. Needless to say, we know the Church is always basically or essentially the same. But, at the same time, we know that our community of Christians has *grown*. And this growth is by no means in terms of only sheer numbers, but more deeply a growth in maturity. This is so because such a way of growth is by experience, and experience makes us more fully aware of our identity, of who

1. This chapter, in its essence, was originally published under the title **Our Living Liturgy** (Chicago: Claretian Publications, 1966) and is reprinted here by permission.
2. Cf. 1 Cor 12:4-31 and **Transformation in Christ**, chaps. 3, 5, 8.

we are. And so, as we live and worship together as the Body of Christ, we more deeply realize what it is to be a member of this Body, what we are to do as Christians, who this Jesus is upon whom we base our lives.

In short, the Church remains *essentially* the same. But in many respects *the Church changes because the Church is alive!* This is why our manner of worship, while it has always remained essentially the same, has so often changed, and will continue to change until the end of time, because it is the worship of a living community.

All of this may be true, but important questions remain: Why are we immersed in an era of sudden change in many aspects of the Church's forms of worship? Why do these things come now, and not another time? What are some of the changes in past eras? And, finally, what may be expected in the future?

If we are to answer any of the above questions adequately, we must have some understanding of the nature of our worship and the changes in form that it has undergone in the past.

When Our Lord told the Disciples at the Last Supper, "Do this in remembrance of me!"[3] he did not provide them with a hefty and detailed Roman Missal, or Gothic architecture, or an intricate system of chant, or many of the other surroundings which contemporary Catholics have remembered as typical of "traditional Catholic worship". All that the Apostolic Church began with were the essentials of the Sacrament of the Eucharist: the matter of the bread and wine, and the specifying words of the Sacrament. We place special emphasis here upon the *words*, because Jesus, in being sacramentally present through his Church, not only provides the matter of the sacraments, but also the

3. Cf. Mt 26:26f; Mk 14:22f; Lk 22:19f.

[4]

words which specify the *meaning* of what is taking place.
So then, we see that our sacramental worship necessarily
consists in large part of *words*. We are aware of the fact
that our participation in this Eucharistic sacrament—most
explicitly our reception of the Body and Blood of Christ in
Holy Communion—expresses our desire to be one with and in
the Lord, to accept our roles as members of this Body of
his which is the Church. But how can we do this unless we
know who it is that we receive? For this reason, the Triune
God reveals himself by means of the *word*, in the lessons of
the Scriptures and in the preaching of the living Church.
But this is not the only role of the word in our worship:
once we begin to grasp some sense of who this Jesus is who
becomes sacramentally present to us, we are often hesitant
and inadequate—unsure of ourselves—in expressing our response to the Word by which he has communicated himself
to us. And so it is, by means of the spoken and sung prayers
of the Church, that Christ through that very Church provides us with words for our responses, enabling us not only
to respond together as a community but also to grow in our
understanding of what our responses should be if we are
to be living members of the Body of Christ.[4]

So it is not unusual to expect that Christians of Apostolic
times placed emphasis on that facet of the liturgy which we
call the "Service of the Word", which was in fact derived
from the Jewish synagogue service, since most of the early
followers of Jesus were Jews.[5] Most of these early Christians,

4. Cf. **Transformation in Christ**, pp. 102f; it should be obvious that this
   is not meant to preclude spontaneity or creativity in the development
   of liturgical texts; cf. this chapter, infra.
5. Barnabas M. Ahern, "The Concept of the Church in Biblical Thought",
   in Proceedings of the Society of Catholic College Teachers of Sacred Doctrine (SCCTSD, now College Theology Society), Vol. 7 (1961),
   p. 36. Also cf. Oscar Cullmann, **Early Christian Worship** (Chicago:
   Regnery, 1953), tr. A. S. Todd and J. B. Torrance, p. 15, and Ac 2:
   42-47.

in fact, since they considered Jesus the fulfillment of Jewish hopes for a Messiah, participated in the Christian Eucharist while continuing their synagogue worship; for them, to be a Christian meant to be a good Jew who accepted Jesus as the Messiah.[6] After Jewish authorities, by means of persecution, made it clear that these Christians were to be rejected by official Judaism, and also after the spread of the Church to the gentiles, the Christians included their own "Service of the Word" in the Eucharistic liturgy. The "Service of the Word" in the synagogue included readings from the Torah (the first five books of the Old Testament, or Pentateuch) and the Prophets; our Christian "Service of the Word", eventually drawing upon its own inspired writings, continues to utilize readings from the Old Testament in addition to the Epistles and Gospels of the New Testament.[7]

The early liturgy of the Church also was often bound up with a meal, called the *agape* in Greek (denoting love). It was at this *agape* meal that the worshipping community shared together in a common feast, symbolizing unity in the love of Christ. Noted liturgical scholars like Josef Andreas Jungmann have pointed out that the Eucharistic celebration was not always necessarily connected with a meal, but that it often was, especially towards the end of the first century.[8]

In the primitive Church, we see that the form of worship will be referred to by two important terms still very much

---

6. Ahern, art. cit.
7. In Mass-liturgies composed in earlier centuries, e.g., certain Lenten Masses, there were three lessons (Old Testament, Epistle, Gospel), but in more recently composed Masses only two. Since the **Ordo Missae** of 1970 the Church in the Roman Rite has been attempting a return to the tradition implied in the earlier arrangement.
8. Josef A. Jungmann, **The Mass of the Roman Rite** (Missarum Sollemnia), one-volume edition tr. F. Brunner, rev. C. Reipe (New York: Benziger Brothers, Inc., 1969), chap. I passim. Also Cf. I Cor 11.

in use today: the *liturgy* and the *Eucharist*. The first term, from the Greek, denotes a public action; the second, likewise from the Greek, means thanksgiving. The latter term, of course, is more specific: while many things are public worship actions, not every worship action is strictly *eucharistic*. The *Eucharistia* (the original form of the Greek word) or thanksgiving prayer was a prayer or series of prayers said by the president of the assembly (celebrant) during the worship-action. In the eucharistic prayers of old, as with those of today, the Christian community thanks God the Father for the very fact of his being a father, for sending his only Son to be our brother and to make us members of his Body, the Church. Furthermore, the Eucharistic Presence of Jesus allows for thanksgiving not only in word but in action, in partaking of the very saving presence for which we give thanks, in Communion. So that, just as Jesus gives himself to us by word and action, we too express to him and to the Father and the Holy Spirit our thanks and willingness to be one with the Trinity both by word and by action. And this we do as members of a worshipping community, not merely as a number of isolated individuals who happen to be in the same place at the same time for the same purpose —for that is not a community but merely a gang or mob. And we see, too, that the very matter or basis which the Lord chooses for this Sacrament is that of a meal, in which members of the community come together in friendship to enjoy God's gifts, and from which those friends come away not only nourished but also drawn into an increasing closeness as members of the Body of Christ. As we said before, Jesus did not provide the Apostles with all the intricate accoutrements of the twentieth-century Mass. How did the Mass come to be as it is now? We shall now attempt to trace some of these developments in our ever-changing, always-the-same liturgy.

The early liturgy was indeed quite spontaneous: the *Eucharistia* or great prayer of thanksgiving (in recent times called the Canon in the Western rites) was said impromptu by the celebrant on most occasions, although ancient documents of the Church in both the Eastern and Western regions show certain canons which evolved into written form and were often used by a celebrant who for some reason did not improvise his own. The same was true of the orations, the prayers said by the celebrant in the name of the community (in recent times called the collect, secret or prayer over the gifts, and the postcommunion). While the Church, in the early centuries, spread throughout the then-known world into both the Eastern and Western regions, the liturgy was always celebrated not only with reverence, but also with *spontaneity*. This meant that the entire worshipping community sang together the acclamations or hymns of the liturgy (excepting those which properly belonged to the celebrant alone), and, of course, no language was used but that of the people. The early liturgy, too, was most often celebrated at a table, and the community stood around the table as the celebrant, facing them, led them in the communal exercise of Eucharistic worship.[9]

Earliest sources indicate that the basic structure of our present Mass-liturgy (e.g., invitatory, Eucharistic prayer, communion) was in widespread use by about A.D. 150. The oldest complete text we find of the Eucharistic prayer is that in the *Apostolic Tradition* of Hippolytus (d. A.D. 235). However, scholars note that we must not consider Hippolytus' documents as *The* Roman Mass of the third century; rather, by this time, there was still no fixed formulary.[10]

9. Jungmann, ibid.
10. Ibid., p. 20: "Hippolytus presents his text only as a suggestion, and expressly stresses the right freely to extemporize a text as a right which remained long in force. This right Hippolytus himself here laid claim to."

So, at this time, while there are fixed statutes concerning the manner of worship, the building of places for worship, etc., and while the basic structure of all the early Eucharistic liturgies is similar, flexibility and spontaneity are still very much in evidence.[11]

Meanwhile, in the East, by the fourth century there were developing liturgical forms based on the *Euchologion* of Bishop Serapion of Thmuis (this emanated from the sphere of influence of Alexandria), or upon the *Apostolic Constitutions* (emanating from Antioch). While we will not explore Eastern liturgical forms in any detail here, we might do well to note that diversity has always been the keynote of liturgical development in the East, so much so that at present there may be counted over a hundred Eastern rites—all Catholic, all united to the Holy See at Rome (having their Orthodox counterparts).[12] By contrast, we shall see, the keynote of liturgical development in the West tended to become uniformity.

By the fourth century, in the West, Latin had replaced Greek as the language of the liturgy because it had replaced Greek as the vernacular.[13] While Latin became the cultural and liturgical language of the Western regions at this time, we must note that the liturgy in the West was still performed in a number of different forms or rites. Of course, the *Roman* liturgy is most familiar to us today, but by the sixth century there had developed such rites as the *Ambrosian* in the area of Milan, Italy;[14] the *Celtic* (used in north-

11. Ibid., passim.
12. Ibid. Also cf. Edward J. Finn, **A Brief History of the Eastern Rites** (Collegeville, Minn.: The Liturgical Press, 1961). The enumeration, of course, depends on whether one groups areas of ritual form together into major categories, or counts all the different variations and subdivisions of rites.
13. Latin began to be used as early as the second century in some areas, e.g., North Africa.
14. The Ambrosian or Milanese rite was preserved in that region.

western Europe but out of use since the eighth century);[15] the *Mozarabic* (a Spanish rite preserved in Toledo);[16] and the *Gallican* (an elaborate Frankish liturgy). The last of these rites, the Gallican, has influenced the development of the Roman Rite to no small degree.

The Gallican liturgy was extremely formalistic, with a different Mass-formulary for each feast of Our Lord or of certain saints, numerous processions, elaborate chants (in later stages) and many orations. At the same time, this rite lacked any real regulating center, and by the eighth century the Roman Rite was often being used in its stead. The Roman Rite, by this time, had become rather formally codified, and found its way into various liturgical books which were the predecessors of the *Missale Romanum*.[17]

By the end of the eighth century, the use of the Roman Rite throughout the West was decreed (by Pepin in 754),[18] but in practice, by this time many of the bishops of France were already substituting the Roman Rite for the Gallican anyway. When the Roman Rite came to be instituted on a large scale in the Frankish regions, however, there was great need of the appropriate liturgical books. But in this age of limited communications media, the books most readily available, and thus likely to be used, were those for the elaborate and solemn papal stational services, which of course were by no means the ordinary daily liturgy at

15. The Celtic rite was hardly a rite in itself, but rather an adaptation of a basically Roman liturgy for missionary use.
16. This rite is reputed to have been preserved on only one altar in a chapel of the Cathedral in Toledo.
17. The separate books for various liturgical functions (e.g., sacramentary, lectionary) exist again today. The **Missale Romanum** came into being out of necessity for the "one-man" Mass or "low Mass" when the celebrant had to take the parts of deacon, subdeacon, **schola cantorum**, etc.
18. Jungmann, p. 56.

Rome! The Frankish liturgical books which were subsequently produced followed the detail of the Roman documents faithfully. However, the Roman Rite found itself developing in a new atmosphere, and thus gained many Gallican forms, e.g., lengthening and multiplying of orations at Mass (we are familiar with one or two; the Gallicans often said seven at a Mass; also many Offertory Prayers come from this period), multiplication of Offertory prayers, a flair for the dramatic and ceremonial (multiple incensations and benedictions) and the poetic ("sequence" chants).

Meanwhile, by the tenth century, the vernacular dialects of the northern regions were becoming very much removed from the Latin of the new Roman Mass (this development had not fully taken place yet while the Gallican liturgy—also a Latin one—was still in use). In fact, Latin was understood by only a small group of educated people (primarily, albeit not exclusively, the clergy), and was largely foreign to the illiterate masses. The vernacular (or "vulgar") languages of the time were not literary languages, i.e., there was no way of committing them to writing—and this in an age of a highly codified written liturgy, centrally controlled (at least in theory) from Rome. It was impossible, then, for the liturgy to remain so codified and highly ordered and at the same time make a transition from Latin to the vernacular.

Also at this time, we must note, some of the laity had such an affinity and held such admiration for things Roman (as did many a cleric) that they actually tended to *prefer* that the Mass remain in Latin rather than be translated into their own language. All things considered, this could probably have been a sort of misguided "cultural snobbishness" or "status-seeking", and it was by no means limited to concerns of religious observance, but manifest also in cultural, financial and governmental attitudes as well, with regard to Rome as focal point in the West.

There was, too, an attitude around and after A.D. 1000 which considered the Mass as a sort of clerical preserve, and there was, therefore, not much lay interest in what has come to be "participation in the Mass". The popular notion saw the Mass not as offered by the People of God with the celebrant as president of their worshipping assembly, but as offered *by* the clergy *for* the laity, who were passive beneficiaries or silent spectators. The celebrant no longer faced his congregation at a banquet table, but faced away from them at an altar built up the wall (or near the rear wall) of the sanctuary, containing a tabernacle as a high throne for the Blessed Sacrament. The sanctuary, to be occupied by the clergy, was at times actually separated from the nave of the church by a wall-like structure (roodscreen)[19] which accented the separation of clergy and laity in the Church and in the liturgy. The laity seldom received Holy Communion, and when they did so (usually at Easter, after arduous Lenten penance) it was outside of the Mass-liturgy, so as to avoid disturbing "the priest's Mass".

During such times, it was not hard to understand that Communion would fail to be at the high-point of the Mass in popular lay piety; its place became taken by the Elevation of the Sacred Species after the Consecration, where the congregation could view the fruits of the Sacrifice performed by the priest in their behalf (there even arose superstitious practices associated with viewing the consecrated and elevated Host or Chalice).

While the laity remained silent in the nave, and the clergy officiated in the sanctuary, another matter altogether

---

19. The roodscreen, intended to insulate the sanctuary (where clerics assisted at Mass and prayed the Office in adverse climates) tended to become elaborate and wall-like, with apertures allowing for congregational viewing of the liturgy (especially in Elevation of the Sacred Species after the Consecration).

was occupying the choir or *schola cantorum:* as the second millennium rolled on, Church music became more elaborate and ornate, less like the simple plainchant or humbler polyphony of old, more divorced from the actions of ministers and congregation. While the celebrant said the *Introit* the choir sang an involved and lengthy *Kyrie;* while he began the Canon they sang an elaborate *Sanctus,* paused for the consecration and elevation of the Sacred Species, then continued with the *Benedictus.*[20] In short, liturgical music almost ceased to become the music of worship and became the music of concert.

As many theologians have noted, the Mass (miraculously, say some) remained the chief source of grace for the Christian community even throughout this awful decline of the liturgy in the West. Christ's definitive sign of love for his Body the Church—his dynamic presence in the Holy Eucharist—remained the focal point of Christian life. Yet, obviously, while the Eucharistic liturgy was essentially the same, it was significantly different from the worship of the early Church. And, to say the least, reforms were in order. One wonders, then, why reforms were not initiated once the state of affairs began to become obvious—say, in the late Middle Ages or the Renaissance.

Liturgical renewal would probably have taken place around the time of the Reformation, had it not been for the turbulent atmosphere of the Reformation itself. Luther and the other reformers had indeed insisted that the liturgy should be restored to earlier and more authentic forms and practices. However, such suggestions suffered precisely because of their very association with the reformers. We must remember that the sixteenth century was not an age of mass

---

20. The **Benedictus** became known as a separate liturgical text in the parlance of Church musicians.

communication like our own, or an age of mass education. This made it even more difficult than it would normally be to distinguish what was being advocated by whom on what grounds and to what end. And Latin, along with other characteristics of liturgical rigidity, somehow became identifying marks of the Church that remained loyal to the papacy. Also, we should point out here, the Council of Trent, which convened in 1545 and met for a period of almost two decades, had to deal with a defense of the whole of Catholic doctrine on redemption, sacraments and authority in the Church. After such an exhaustive agenda—still not completed to satisfaction—few Council fathers were about to launch a program of extensive liturgical renewal (although Trent did deal directly with some abuses in the liturgy which seemed to require immediate rectification). Suffering the wounds of a violent and painful crisis, the Church was in no mood for a far-reaching series of reforms in liturgy—especially in an age when such reforms would be far harder to implement than in our own. Frankly, it must here be noted that many began to confuse the substance of the Catholic faith with its accidents, the aspects of the Church's life that can change with those that cannot. And so, in times of interdenominational misunderstanding and mutual fear and suspicion, many Catholics and others grew to believe that the use of Latin in the liturgy was somehow an article of dogma, something that had always been (forgetting, of course, the early history of the Church) and always would have to be.[21]

Also, in reaction to the theories of Protestant reformers, many Catholics began to stress the validity of orders and other sacraments, especially the reality of Christ's presence in the Eucharist, to the point where personal involvement

21. Cf. **Transformation in Christ**, chaps. 1, 2, 5.

was strongly *de*-emphasized. Even in our own century, we sometimes hear such expressions as "Just as long as Mass is said and I'm there, I get just as much grace—whether or not I sing or pray or whatever I do!" What is really the case, of course, is that the Lord is present in any valid Mass, but that our growth in grace is intensified by a fuller consciousness of the sacrament we are celebrating—that we cannot merely be satisfied by nothing more than validity itself.[22]

We are familiar, now, with changes that took place in the Mass from the earliest centuries up to the time after the Council of Trent,[23] and many developments in attitudes toward liturgy. We see that many of these developments were good, and others cried out for improvement. But, we ask, why did such momentous changes as heralded in our own century take place *when* they did? We know that ours is an age in which communications and similar facilities are readily available to aid the work of men involved in sweeping changes and their proclamation, and that newer, better and simply *more* tools are available to the scholars and Fathers of the Church. But there is a deeper reason why this renewal of the liturgy should find itself in the twentieth century.

That reason lies in the Scriptures. Our liturgy is Biblically-rooted, and our Sacraments are events specified by the Word of God. Now we see the import of this in the latter nineteenth century. The era of which we speak here was one of great controversy regarding the interpretation of the Scrip-

22. Ibid., Chapter 5, especially pp. 98-99.
23. This is obviously a skeletal outline of the major trends; for a complete historical treatment cf. Jungmann, op. cit., and also his **Public Worship: A Survey** (Collegeville, Minn.: The Liturgical Press, 1957) tr. Fr. Clifford Howell and **The Early Liturgy to the Time of Gregory the Great** (Notre Dame, Ind.: The University of Notre Dame Press, 1959), tr. F. Brunner. There were a few attempts at liturgical renewal between the sixteenth and nineteenth centuries, but these were superficial and short-lived.

[15]

2

tures. Critical scholars like Wellhausen and Harnack, and the rationalists like Renan and Loisy, proposed theories and questions which sent Protestant and Catholic scholars alike back to their Bibles. Also, of course, the 1859 publication of Charles Darwin's theory of evolution by natural selection in *The Origin of Species* was a significant point in this age of growing theological ferment.

Because our faith *is* so Scripturally-based, any renewal in Biblical studies would necessarily bring with it a rebirth of theological studies in general. And, since our liturgy is so Scripturally-rooted, such a Biblical renaissance would necessarily bring with it a liturgical renaissance. This period of scholarly reawakening, then, brought into a more prominent light the history of theology, the Church as Christ's Body, of the liturgy as a *communal* activity, and the practices of the early Church and the history of the liturgy were coming into sharper focus. One great atmosphere of liturgical and general theological development would surely be the monasteries, where there were great opportunities not only for Biblical, theological and historical scholarship, but also for a liturgical life centering in the celebration of the Eucharist and the praying of the Divine Office daily. So it was that, in the context of a monastic life that focused on the liturgy, the liturgical renewal of the modern era began to flourish at monasteries like Solesmes, paving the way for the reforms of the twentieth century.

The Anatomy of Renewal
The Twentieth Century (to 1963)

THE TWENTIETH CENTURY is pivotal so far as the reform of the liturgy in the West is concerned. The heightened Biblical and historical scholarship which began late in the nineteenth century came to a crescendo in the twentieth, and its results began to manifest themselves in a variety of practical effects.

In 1903 Pope St. Pius X issued his famous *Motu proprio* condemning numerous abuses in the liturgy, principally those trends which isolated the laity from participating intelligently in the Mass.[1] One of these was bad liturgical music, which had degenerated into an irrelevant concert. Pius, then, insisted on a return to the spirit of the liturgy in earlier times, not out of antiquarianism for its own sake, but in the hope that this would put the Church back onto a path of more authentic tradition in her expression of worship.

The gist of Pope Pius X's reasoning was that the symbols in the Roman liturgy could best be perceived as symbols if they were a bit less cluttered. Thus his emphasis on Gregorian Chant, wherein the melodic patterns were unquestionably vehicles for the Word of God in the liturgy, and not vice versa. The plainchant of the Church could serve to focus the mind and heart of man directly on the Lord and his teachings, it was felt, whereas the more elaborate, more recent, compositions of music for the liturgy ran the risk of distraction.

Pius X's desire that all have access to the riches of the

1. **Tra le Sollecitudini,** ASS XXXVI (1903): 329-39.

Eucharistic liturgy was certainly behind his subsequent lowering of the requisite age for first holy communion in the Roman Rite from twelve years of age to seven. This was a part of his larger effort to encourage frequent reception of the Eucharist by the laity.[2]

Pius X well typifies the spirit of the liturgical renewal in the early twentieth century in that this spirit was by no means superficial or limited to the niceties of the liturgical arts. At the outset, the "Pope of the Holy Eucharist" made clear that his intention was to draw the members of the Church to the graces available to them in the Lord's own sacrificial meal. Insofar as reforms in various aspects of liturgical expression, such as music, could facilitate that end, the Holy Father encouraged these. A similar spirit prevailed during the pontificate of Pope Pius XI,[3] who is remembered for the apostolic constitution *Divini cultus*[4] which underscored the points stressed by his predecessor.

A cursory glance at the documents issued under Popes Pius X and XI might lead one to believe that they were preoccupied with the topic of Church music and the Gregorian revival. In reality, such was not the case. However, it might appear that way since liturgical music was perhaps the most obvious area where reform was not only needed but possible. Any other undertaking of reform for the Roman Rite would necessitate a serious theological re-examination of the Church and the Eucharistic liturgy for application to the contemporary situation, in the light of sound biblical and historical scholarship. This was to come later, at the Second Vatican Council, but it was not able to happen earlier, when many of the necessary theological and historical

2. Cf. **ASS** XXXVII (1905): 425-32, 613-25.
3. 1922-39.
4. **AAS** XXI (1929): 33-41.

resources were in the process of development.[5] During the pontificate of Pope Pius XI, the monumental work of Josef Andreas Jungmann on the history of the Roman Mass-liturgy had yet to make its impact on the Church; much of the liturgical spadework of the Benedictines in Europe and in Minnesota was in adolescence; the preparation of the bishops and clergy for a new liturgical awareness was in its infancy. Also, it must surely have been remembered that to even scratch the surface of the Roman liturgy was a herculean effort, as was the case in the lengthy and complex deliberations of the Council of Trent.[6] While it was indeed true that Trent was rife with difficulties that did not obtain during the time of Pius X and XI, both pontiffs and their contemporaries must have appreciated the massive problems that would be involved in even a minor rubrical overhaul, and were understandably reluctant to commit the Church to such a task. But *musical* renewal for the liturgy required little or none of that. If the worshipping assembly were to cease being a place where the laity were silent spectators at a garish pageant or opera, perhaps a purification of liturgical music would be the logical place to begin.

In an age when music for the liturgy seems characterized by an almost barren simplicity, it may be hard to appreciate the state of liturgical music in the early years of this very century. The musical performances at Mass were of such an ostentatious nature that people commonly attended Mass at a particular church simply to hear the music, replete with many-voiced choir and various instrumentalists and soloists. Devout churchgoers often had to make their way into their worship-places in competition with unbelieving

---

5. Cf. George Devine, **Our Living Liturgy** (Chicago: Claretian Publications, 1966), p. 17.
6. **Ibid.**, p. 18.

dilettantes.[7] Composers had become accustomed to competing with each other in the effort to produce elaborate and dramatic statements of the themes of the Mass ordinary. For some, this was doubtless an expression of piety. For many others, however, it was merely a great challenge to a musician to "write a Mass". The first Christmas Midnight Mass celebrated in the new St. Ignatius Church in San Francisco, in 1914, offered a printed program which advertised violinists and opera singers in the sanctuary; such a performance was by no means atypical of the musical menu for major feasts in Catholic churches.[8]

Lest it be thought that the Church was about to overreact to abuses in liturgical music, we should note that mere gaud was not the extent of the concern expressed in Rome. Indeed, Rome itself is the *locus* of the anecdote in which an Italian cardinal was celebrant of a solemn Mass when the choir was singing a lengthy *Credo* which developed its musical theme at one point by juxtaposing the words *genitum, non factum,* with *factum, non genitum.*[9] Of course, the second set of words directly contradicted the original words of the Creed and was in that way a clear statement of direct heresy. Even this seemed less important to His Eminence than did the excessive length of the musical rendition, for as the choir continued to sing *genitum, non factum; factum, non genitum* the cardinal suddenly rose from the *sedilia* and intoned at the top of his voice: *Factum*

---

7. Cf. H. A. Reinhold, **The Dynamics of Liturgy** (New York: MacMillan, 1961), passim.
8. My father was present that Christmas Eve at St. Ignatius and recalled that the musical program was essentially characteristic of the time.
9. The words **genitum, non factum** refer to the Second Person of the Trinity having been born (generated), not made; the reverse order of words, **factum, non genitum,** would of course have the opposite meaning, that the Word was created, not generated, and this would directly contradict the Christological dogmas of the Church.

vel non factum, Dominus vobiscum![10] and the Mass continued without further singing of the *Credo.*

The Gregorian renewal, then, was the harbinger of other reforms to come in the Roman Mass-liturgy, the first of several purifications to make their mark on the liturgical experience of Catholics. And underlying it was a subtle, steady development in liturgical scholarship, rooted in the historical and biblical renaissance that had begun in the second half of the nineteenth century.[11]

It was that type of scholarship that began to be evident in the documents of Pius X, the apostolic constitution *Divini cultus* of Pius XI, but much more so in the two famous encyclical letters of Pius XII, *Mystici Corporis Christi* and *Mediator Dei.* The former was issued in 1943[12] (the same year as *Divino afflante Spiritu,* regarded as the magna carta for modern Biblical scholarship; perhaps this is no coincidence). In *Mystici Corporis Christi* Pius re-introduced into the general Catholic consciousness the doctrine of St. Paul that presents the Church as the Body of Christ: a visible, active, effective presence of Christ in the world in which the various members (as with the members of a physical body) are *interdependent.*[13] This would seem quite familiar to many Catholics today, as well it did to those of antiquity. But for some time, the doctrine had not been stressed in the ordinary preaching and teaching of the Church. More importantly, the liturgical experience of Catholics in the West had been one of anything *but* inter-

---

10. The Latin *vel* translates into English as "or". **Dominus vobiscum** was the intonation to be given by the celebrant at the completion of the **Credo.** So the cardinal was saying, in effect, "made or not made, let's get on with the Mass!"
11. Cf. Devine, op. cit., p. 21.
12. AAS XXXV (1943): 193-248;
13. Cf. I Corinthians 12:4-31; Ephesians 4:1-5:20.

dependency or community in Christ. In truth, the celebration of the Mass in the Roman Rite had allowed the average lay Catholic to believe that the meeting-place of the Christian assembly was not that at all, but rather a convenient place where numerous members of the Church could have their one-to-one relationships with God taken care of in the same location at the same time for the convenience of the overburdened priest. This type of thing, obviously, went hand-in-hand with a failure to appreciate the social dimensions and demands of the Gospel message: salvation was seen as an individual matter, and corporate responsibility did not enter the narrow perspective afforded by such a viewpoint.

It logically followed that there had built up in the Catholic consciousness (and surely in the Catholic subconsciousness) no great receptivity to the notion of the Mass as a communal celebration, let alone the corollary which would mandate social concern as a natural outgrowth of the sharing in Christ's eucharistic banquet. The liturgical movement that began to enter its adulthood during the later years of Pius XII's pontificate would attempt to change that, but much pre-evangelization would be in order first. We had become a Church full of people—priests and laity alike—who sincerely believed that no one should ever talk in Church excepting the priest; much reconditioning would be needed before such a people could become at all comfortable with "dialogue Mass". We had come to intuit that any sort of informality or emotional expression in church was out of place; such a people would find it difficult to join in the singing of a communion hymn. Thus it was that a theological articulation had to come before liturgical renovation itself.

Among priests who read encyclicals, *Mystici Corporis Christi* made no small impact. For some it was a personal vindication. One can imagine the scholarly Jesuit in Boston who was criticized by his superiors for preaching a sermon on the Mystical Body of Christ during the late 1930s now taking consolation in the words of the Holy See. But to suppose that all priests read encyclicals is no more realistic than to assume that all Americans read the President's speeches in the New York *Times,* or even that all Congressmen read the *Congressional Record.* This is not to imply slovenliness on the part of the clergy. In reality, the failure of Pius' encyclicals to make as much of an impression as desired is in large measure connected with the particular vision of piety-in-practice that was popular among the American clergy at the time, and of a number of other priests around the world as well, namely that the average priest had all he could do to keep up with the daily practical chores of his ministry, and that an encyclical letter which explained complex theological matters would be of little pastoral import, so long as the faithful Catholic implicitly assented to whatever the Holy Father taught. Furthermore, it is a technical fact that encyclical letters, strictly speaking, are written by the Bishop of Rome to his fellow bishops in the various dioceses of the Church around the world. Thus, an encyclical which had great significance for the priests or lay people in general would presumably be promulgated by the local ordinary. Finally, one must entertain the notion of many a hard-pressed bishop relying on his own *periti* for a reading of an encyclical, duly receiving it and noting it, and sincerely feeling that further attention to the matter would not be necessary.

For the reasons listed above, the liturgical movement of the twentieth century did not begin as a genuine grass-roots phenomenon. It was, instead, generated first by the *cognoscenti* of the Church, in European monasteries and then in American abbeys and seminaries which enjoyed European

connections. So it was that the center of American liturgical
aggiornamento would be at the Benedictine abbey of St.
John in Minnesota. So, too, would Germans lead the renewal among the clergy: Hans Ansgar Reinhold, Reynold
Hillenbrand, Martin Hellriegel, these were the pioneers of
liturgical renewal in the United States—not the predomi-
nantly Irish clergy who were unfamiliar with what was happening on the Continent. This meant that the two Coasts
of the United States would lag behind the Middle West in
their understanding of what was coming to be. The Pacific
and Atlantic seaboards, in time, would know young Jesuits
who had studied at Innsbruck or Louvain or Institut Catho-
lique de Paris, but these regions would be far behind the
center of the country in their appreciation of matters liturgical.[14] The diocesan clergy in the Middle West would be
influenced by Hillenbrand ("Hilly", as many a Chicago
priest affectionately calls him) or Hellriegel; on the Coasts,
the secular priest would not be so fortunate, but he might
stumble across an issue of *Worship* (originally *Orate,
Fratres*) from St. John's Abbey or hear a talk somewhere
that might help him understand what was going on liturgically.

The movement was slow. But there would be more indig-
enous clergy who would communicate the liturgical reform
of the Church in the pulpit, the seminary, the college. Men
like Gerald Ellard, William Leonard, Gerard Sloyan and
Frederick McManus would make their impact on seminarians, students, some religious, even some fellow priests.
But the impact had yet to be made on the diocesan or
parish level. One reason for this was the separation of the
Church's *cognoscenti* from the practical grass-roots situ-

14. Cf. **Transformation in Christ,** chap. 2.

ation. The intellectual in the Church, then as now, has too often been on the sidelines, able to comment on the passing scene but unable to influence it directly. The men who led the liturgical renewal in the early years were generally neither pastors nor bishops. Hellriegel was an exception, being a pastor; likewise HAR; and "Hilly" was a pastor after years as a seminary rector. But by and large, the liturgical experts were professors in seminaries and colleges. Their impact was in the classroom, the lecture hall, the occasional retreat or speaking engagement, and perhaps in publication among their scholarly peers. But they were not in a position to directly influence the course of development of liturgical attitudes or actions in the parishes and dioceses of America. Even their publications of a popular nature (pamphlets) were subject to a sort of prior receptivity on the grass-roots level. In retrospect, we would certainly be loath to have lost the contribution which such great scholars and liturgists made in the places where they did, though we cannot help but lament the fact that their base of operations was not wider.

One factor which must not go unnoticed here is another dimension of the monasticism which characterized the earlier stages of the modern liturgical movement. The liturgical leaders in this country were not deprived of pastorates or bishoprics out of any malice or discrimination. The simple fact is that most of them were not secular clergy, but rather members of monastic or semi-monastic religious orders. Thus, the same circumstance which allowed them to combine a life of liturgical and theological scholarship with a life of communal liturgical celebration also managed to limit their spheres of influence to those places where the religious orders they belonged to held sway: they could not generally be bishops or pastors, but could be professors or abbots or authors. This would make for an influence which would be gradual and indirect, but lasting nonetheless.

The monastic flavor of the early renewal of the liturgy in this century meant a grounding in thorough scholarship. This was necessary since the Church at large had yet to become really aware of its own liturgical history and its ability to change in the future as it had in the past. Again, it is necessary to point out the singular influence of the Benedictines at St. John's who popularized a great deal of fine liturgical scholarship through their Liturgical Press and their periodicals (*Orate, Fratres*–later *Worship,* and *Sponsa Regis*–later *Sisters Today*). The St. John's Benedictines made it possible for the parish priest, the religious, the seminarian or student to digest the historical, Biblical, theological and aesthetic studies related to liturgy that came out of the centers of Europe, as well as papal teachings on these subjects, in a fashion which was readily accessible and inexpensive. This was a substantial and lasting contribution of inestimable value to the life of the modern American Church.

Also, the monastic spirit of the liturgical renewal brought with it a very strong Scriptural basis. Part of this, of course, can be taken to denote the ongoing Biblical studies that went on in monasteries and abbeys, and which were surely found surfacing in the liturgical renewal. Another aspect of this was the importance of the Divine Office in monastic communities, where the Hours of the day were seen as radiating from the central liturgical celebration of the Eucharist. This meant an increased sense of the import of the Service of the Word in the eucharistic liturgy itself, and as reflected in the Scriptural selections that would be utilized throughout the Office for the day, week or liturgical season. The ideal that would be sought, then, would be a life which was not merely preoccupied with the fine points of liturgical form, but which used the structures and forms of the liturgy so as to inspire and enrich a life of prayerful activity in the world, feeding on the liturgy (Mass *and* Office) as the daily bread which sustained the Christian life.[15]

The liturgical movement in this century has come to be known for its simplicity of style: the sublime plainchant, the uncluttered "monkish" atmosphere of the renewal, the clean, streamlined character of much modern liturgical art and architecture. But this was not always the case, for the earlier attempts at highlighting liturgical forms, symbols and meanings became obfuscated by the multiplicity of forms, symbols and meanings available. So it was with the first editions of the Saint Andrew Missal,[16] or with Pius Parsch's *The Church's Year of Grace*,[17] where symbols and applications abounded to the point of virtual confusion, in some cases. This was a necessary stage of the development. The Church had for so long ignored some of these symbols, meanings, connections that it was necessary to somehow raise the sleeping giant, and in so doing there was not adequate distinction between those elements that were of central import and those which were more tangential. But the economy that was needed would come soon enough, and only after the new appreciation of our rich liturgical heritage had loomed larger than life itself could it cut itself down to manageable size.

Probably the greatest single characteristic in the liturgical movement at the grass roots during the early twentieth century was the popular introduction of altar-missals adapted for use by the laity. In the recent past, i.e., as recently as even the nineteenth century, the laity was not allowed to possess the text of the Mass in the ver-

---

15. If another reference to the Order of St. Benedict may be allowed, this author is inclined to recall their motto **ora et labora** in this context.
16. Later editions became less elaborate and cluttered.
17. Collegeville, Minn.: The Liturgical Press, 1959.

nacular. After a time, the publication of these texts for the laity became permissible—even in "vulgar" tongues, and the hand-missal came into its own.[18] These miniatures of the *Missale Romanum* used by the celebrant at the altar contained the texts of the Mass ordinary (usually *verso* in Latin and *recto* in the vernacular) and the propers of at least major feasts—oftentimes all propers or at least all the basic Mass-proper *schemata* (arranged bilingually as above, or sometimes in the vernacular only). This made it possible for the lay member of the congregation to "follow the Mass" by reading the prayers as the celebrant read them in his own Missal at the altar, alternating between the Ordinary and Proper parts of the Mass. Descriptions of the rubrics which governed the celebrant's movements about the sanctuary (often accompanied by pictures) helped the worshipper in the pew to "pace" his following of the liturgy in his hand-missal.

The hand-missal which flourished in this country for about twenty years before the early 1960s ushered in the *aggiornamento* of Vatican II would appear today to be no more than a rather cumbersome and artificial measure, surely no more than a stopgap. In their time, hand-missals were considered a bother to carry, a mystery to decipher (however easy their editors tried to render them) and an exercise in frustration generally (a ribbon marker going astray and losing the place, or the celebrant reading his own Missal three times faster than his lay congregant could). For all that, the hand-missal was a great step forward for the liturgical movement in the early twentieth-century. Before the introduction of the hand-missal, the faithful at

18. When my parents were married in San Francisco on January 27, 1940, my father gave my mother a Missal as a gift and they were still considered somewhat new then.

Mass had no unifying focus for prayer. Some said the Rosary or other favorite prayers of private devotion. Some read prayerbooks (a generic term in which hand-missals later came to be included). Some attempted to meditate. Some, like their forebears of centuries ago (in the medieval times, surely) gazed about the Church and learned little lessons in the Faith from the statuary, the stained-glass windows, the sculpted back-altar, or the embroidered design on the back of the celebrant's chasuble. The hand-missal did not immediately facilitate devotion or eliminate distraction (for a time, it no doubt accounted for its own share of it), and there were many Catholics who would never use it (often following a devotional avenue which, for them, might have been more efficacious). But the hand-missal managed to underscore the idea of the Mass as the prayer of the entire Christian community—not just the celebrant—and thus as a prayer in which the entire Community of Christ should participate (even if only in a silent, spiritual sense for the time being). It helped to pave the way for the day when the congregation would be asked to follow and join in the prayers and responses of the Mass (often using a latter-day crutch known as a "Missalette").

At an intermediate stage between the silent use of the hand-missal and the initiation of the post-Conciliar participated liturgy was the "dialogue Mass" or community *Missa Recitata*.[19] (Some of the later hand-missals were marked for congregational participation in such a Mass.) This was an application of papal urgings that the participation of the Faithful in the Mass be not only spiritual and interior, but externally vocal as well, in light of liturgical scholarship

---

19. "Recited Mass" or "Read Mass". **Missa Recitata** booklets were published in the 1940s for school and parish use by the Jesuits at The Queen's Work in St. Louis.

which emphasized the fact that most of the Mass-prayers said by the acolytes really belonged to the congregation as a whole and were said by the acolytes only as representatives of the congregation. The "dialogue Mass", then, called upon the congregation to resume their role in the praying of these common acclamations. This could be done in stages, ranging from the simpler responses *(Amen; Et cum spiritu tuo)*[20] to the longer prayers of the Mass *(Gloria; Credo)*. In many a parish, sincere pastors and parishioners attempted the "dialogue Mass" and found it wanting: the Latin pronunciation was a stumbling-block for many in the congregation; the recitation of a foreign tongue in drill-team fashion was seen by many worshippers as a distraction from worship, not an aid; the energy and enervation required for the implementation of "dialogue Mass" often seemed to serve no purpose or achieve no end save compliance with the mind of the Church in the 1940s and 1950s. So it was that many more parishes never tried the "dialogue Mass" at all, and they were probably none the poorer for it, except that they missed out on two "fringe benefits" that attended the "dialogue Mass": a concrete experience of sacrifice for the sake of the self-renewing Church, and an object lesson in the futility of renewing the liturgy without introducing the vernacular.

As part of the Gregorian revival, choirs were being en-

20. This was categorized as "first degree" participation in the **Missa Recitata**, according to the norms of the **Instruction for American Pastors on Sacred Music and the Sacred Liturgy**, issued by the Sacred Congregation of Rites under Pope Pius XII on September 3, 1958. This document, popularly referred to then as "the September Instruction", became in effect a basic "handbook" for liturgists and pastors during the late 1950s and early 1960s. It was, in fact, issued because of a number of queries in the U.S. concerning the permissibility of various liturgical forms and techniques. Cf. William J. Leonard, ed., **The Instruction for American Pastors on Sacred Music and the Sacred Liturgy** (Boston: McLaughlin and Reilly, Inc., 1959).

couraged to perform music which was simpler and more in keeping with the renewed spirit of the liturgy. This did not always mean limiting the musical repertoire to Gregorian Chant. Indeed, many "Gregorianists" advocated a happy marriage between the venerable chant, the more representative music from the ages (e.g., Palestrina) and some modern composers as well (this was to encourage the performance of composers like Flor Peeters and Jean Langlais). Among the new hymnals occasioned by the Gregorian revival, perhaps none became so famous or so widely used as the *Saint Gregory Hymnal* under the editorship of Nicola A. Montani.[21] This was a combination of music from various periods with a number of simple Gregorian chants which could be utilized not only by an average parish choir, but could eventually be sung by even a congregation. The *Saint Gregory* has been criticized—and I think rightly so—for an excessive reliance on some "modern" (late nineteenth and early twentieth century) compositions of a most saccharine character, but it offered to the Church in America a number of benefits not otherwise available at the time: a wide selection of hymns and motets for use at Mass, in addition to Ordinaries and Propers which rendered the Gregorian revival accessible at least in part to the typical community of worshippers. One way in which this was effected was by the printing of Gregorian melodies in modern notation, rather than the four-line staff and squarish *neum* and *punctum* which so bewildered the average Catholic who dared look into a *Kyriale* or *Liber Usualis*.[22] Another was the encouragement of simple chants (though these came to be used to excess): *Missa de Angelis, Kyrie Orbis Factor* and

---

21. Nicola A. Montani, ed., **The Saint Gregory Hymnal** (Philadelphia: St. Gregory Guild, Inc., 1920, 1922, 1940).
22. Benedictines of Solesmes, comp., **The Liber Usualis** (Tournai, Belgium: Descleé & Co., 1952).

Lux et Origo, and so forth, in addition to psalm-tone settings (especially tone 8g) for the Proper parts of the Mass.

As implied above, the next logical step after the "dialogue Mass" and the acclimation of choirs and organists to the Gregorian renewal would be congregational participation in the Mass chants. This, too, was in line with papal desires, although it was tried seldom and succeeded far less often. One obstacle (which still prevails a decade after the liturgical reforms of Vatican II) is the tendency of American Catholics to be spectators rather than participants. This can be seen in a variety of life-situations which surely transcend religion. One chief example of this, of course, is American sports— spectator sports prevail, as opposed to athletics requiring direct participation. Even the national anthem at the ball game is usually sung by a professional (or played on a recording) while the thousands of fans listen mutely (nonetheless patriotic in their silence). The tendency of Americans not to be a vocal people or a musical people *en masse* is compounded in the instance of American Catholics, especially insofar as these are influenced by the Irish-American religious heritage. The Irish, more than any other Catholic people, are most reluctant to utter a sound in Church. This is partially due to a rather skewed notion of reverence which certainly does not afflict such warmer people as the Latins or Italians, but there is a good historical reason as well: the Irish are heavily steeped in the tradition of the "hedge Masses" where the Sacrifice had to be celebrated covertly and quietly so as to avoid detection by persecutors of Irish Catholics in the old country—thus no one spoke at Mass excepting the priest (and anyone delegated by him to respond), and in no case above a whisper, lest the "hedge Mass" be discovered by the enemy. Thus, a reluctance to be vocal—let alone sing—is part and parcel of the American

Catholic experience, especially with an Irish dominance.

Add to that reticence the problems of music in a foreign language. Here is compounded the original problem that tended to make "dialogue Mass" so terribly difficult and frustrating. Usually, a priest did not attempt to lead his people in spoken *or* sung participation in the Latin Mass; if he did, his valiant effort was surely the endeavor of an underdog. When there was success in a parish, it was usually quite limited, and it was usually due to leadership from a cadre within the congregation: in the case of spoken response, that would usually mean the altar boys, who had learned the Mass responses, and would only need to slow their pace so as to lead their fellow lay members of the congregation; in the instance of sung prayer, this would of course mean the choir (or *schola cantorum,* in the proper sense), which would typically sing behind the congregation (in the physical arrangement of the church, at least) and hopefully stimulate their participation.

So far as sung response was concerned, one chief factor was repetition. This led to some interesting notions concerning "easy" and "hard" musical selections. For instance, *Credo III*[23] is one of the more difficult pieces of chant, melodically, yet is commonly acknowledged by Catholics as one of the "easier" ones. The reason is that it was the most widely used of the Gregorian creeds during the 1940s and 1950s, and thus quite familiar to Catholic worshippers who heard it from their choirs repeatedly. (The same principle applies in hymnody: ask any Catholic which is easier, "Holy God We Praise Thy Name" or "Praise God from Whom All Blessings Flow"; the former hymn, being far more familiar, will be specified as "easy" and the latter

23. I am using here the traditional enumeration as found in the **Liber Usualis.**

"hard"—musically, the opposite is true!)[24]

By the time efforts at community *Missa Recitata* and *Missa Cantata* in the United States had reached their peak in the early 1960s, those parishes where they had been minimally successful had hopefully cultivated some sensitivity to the communal nature of Eucharistic worship, and the necessity of interior and exterior participation in the liturgy (even if the mechanics of external participation were a distraction for a time). Moreover, such worshipping communities had a sense of making difficult change for the sake of the Church as it became more the Church. This would stand them in good stead in the *aggiornamento* that was to come in the wake of the Second Vatican Council. But the drill-team mechanics of congregational *Missa Recitata* or *Missa Cantata* were in themselves far from salutary for the development of liturgical piety and vitality, and any advantage to be found in their use would likely be as minimal as outlined above.

When liturgical piety and vitality did develop in the parishes of America before Vatican II, it was likely because the encyclical letters and instructions of the Holy See and the scholarship of theologians and liturgists were being studied and interpreted and applied not simply mechanically, but intelligently, critically and creatively. To the credit of the Church in America, there exist some fine examples of this, a few of which are worth mention in this brief treatment.

One of these examples surely involves the permission included in the 1958 *Instruction for American Pastors on Sacred Music and the Sacred Liturgy*[25] to capitalize on the

24. The terms "easy" and "hard" are obviously being used comparatively here; in the realm of "secular" music, an example of the same point is the Star Spangled Banner.
25. Cf. Leonard, ed., op. cit.

potentialities of "popular religious song" in "low" Masses. To appreciate the ramifications of this subtlety, it is necessary to acknowledge the *Instruction*'s reiteration of the principle that (with exceptions like the Greek *Kyrie*) the only liturgical language of the Roman Rite is Latin, and thus Latin is the language in which all properly liturgical music for the Rite exists. English or other vernacular hymns, however praiseworthy, were not really "liturgical music", in the proper and strict sense in which that phrase was then understood. These, rather, were "popular religious song". They could not be used at a *Missa Cantata* (or "high Mass"); only Latin could be used there (hymns before or after Mass, e.g., processional or recessional, excepted).[27] But in a "low Mass" (in which no singing took place *officially*, i.e., according to the strict rubrics of the liturgy), popular religious song could be utilized to encourage the pious devotion of the Faithful. In many a parish and in other situations (e.g., schools, colleges and the like) this was used to emulate the German tradition of *Betsingmesse* ("pray-and-sing Mass"), where the congregation participated in Mass prayers and hymns in the vernacular while the celebrant read his prayers from the *Missale Romanum* in Latin.[26] This made it possible for the congregation to sing in English an entrance hymn, Offertory hymn, Communion psalm or hymn and recessional or thanksgiving hymn.[27] It even allowed for a congregation to sing the "Propers" of the Mass by choosing vernacular

---

26. Cf. **Transformation in Christ,** pp. 22, 40. This immemorial custom in Germany was an exception to the prohibition of vernacular tongues in the Roman Mass.
27. Processional hymns technically took place before Mass began; likewise, recessional hymns technically took place after Mass ended (for the same reason, the "Prayers After Mass" introduced by Pope Leo XIII —and suppressed by Pope John XXIII—could be in the vernacular, since they were after Mass).

settings of the appropriate Psalms (especially with the advent of composers like Gelineau and Somerville, and later Fitzpatrick). Finally, as the pre-Conciliar liturgical movement was reaching its conclusion, it was even possible (with a cooperative celebrant) for a congregation to utilize vernacular settings of the Mass Ordinary (*Kyrie, Gloria, Creed, Sanctus, Agnus Dei* and even versicles and responses) as these were being developed by Dennis Fitzpatrick.[28]

The chief weakness of the accommodated *Betsingmesse* was that it tended to effect a separation between the celebrant (bound to the Latin *Missale Romanum*) and the congregation (following vernacular prayers and hymns). Also, some felt, the central importance of the priest's role was being clouded by the new prominence of the person who led the vernacular hymns or prayers of the congregation (although the *Instruction* allowed for commentators and lectors, there was some reluctance to accept these, and also some controversy as to whether such persons leading a *Betsingmesse* corresponded properly to the descriptions of commentator and lector outlined in the *Instruction*).[29] For reasons like these, and also owing to the still unresolved Latin-vs.-vernacular tensions in the Church of the early 1960s, the days just before the Council saw the arming of disparate camps in the liturgical arena.

One camp, dedicated to preserving the *status quo,* made frequent citations of Pope John's 1962 document *Veter-*

28. Fitzpatrick's musical settings of the Mass texts in English were intended for eventual use in his **Demonstration English Mass LP** recording and his **Demonstration English Liturgy Altar Missal** (Evanston, Ill.: Friends of the English Liturgy, 1963), both of which were sent to the English-speaking Bishops to help them settle questions of vernacular liturgy during the second session of the Second Vatican Council in 1963. However, prior to this specific use, choir-masters who had known and worked with Fitzpatrick were using his material in and around Chicago and Milwaukee in 1960-1963, especially at daily Masses for parochial school children (sometimes affectionately referred to as **Fitzmesse**).
29. Cf. Leonard, ed., op. cit.

um sapientia,[30] interpolating into it a prohibition of agitation for a vernacular liturgy. Some of these further cited the difficulties of congregational participation in a Latin liturgy as reason to delay any attempts at it "until the people are ready", all the while discouraging efforts to help the people *get* ready.

Another camp was dedicated to carrying out what they understood as the will of the Holy See regarding congregational involvement in and appreciation of the Sacred Liturgy in the Roman Rite. This meant that they took seriously (and perhaps too literally) the *desiderata* expressed in the 1958 *Instruction* concerning the "degrees" and "stages" of participation in the Mass by way of community *Missa Cantata* and *Missa Recitata.* They would campaign for—or at least cooperate with—congregational recitation of the Mass prayers, or singing of the liturgical chants, but they would not go along with measures which they saw as detrimental to the unity of the Church, e.g., attempts at an indirect introduction of vernacular worship through the permission of the 1958 *Instruction* (vernacular hymns at Mass, *Betsingmesse,* etc.)

Still a third camp understood the will of the Church a little differently. This group tended to enjoy the leadership of the liturgical experts themselves, and to interpret the spirit and methodologies of the liturgical movement in such wise as to be as creative as possible within the parameters of the instructions, permissions and limitations given by the Church either in Rome or in particular localities. This group also tended to regard congregational participation in a Latin Mass with increasing frustration, and began more

30. This apostolic constitution (AAS LIV (1962): 129-35) issued under Pope John XXIII was intended to reinforce the study of Latin in seminaries; Latinists tended to see in it a suppression of arguments for the vernacularization of the liturgy.

and more to circumvent the Latin liturgy by resorting to "low" services that would allow for such vernacular techniques as embodied in the *Betsingmesse*. These individuals, too, viewed reform of the liturgy with a certain global vision; for them, it would hardly be enough to effect external participation and internal involvement in the liturgy without re-ordering priorities of liturgical art and architecture to conform to the spirit of liturgical renewal (hence conical vestments, altar-centered and almost statueless churches, enamel-covered chalices, and most of all, altars facing the people).

As the early sixties approached the mid-sixties, it was clear that the ideological victory in the liturgical *aggiornamento* of the Church would go to the last of these camps. Their leaders would be the ones who would influence the Council deliberations at Rome, whose books would sell in the Catholic shops, who would be invited to give the lectures and retreats and explain the "new liturgy". Their ideas would typify that "new liturgy", and not the Latinist or *status quo* point of view. But minds and hearts are not changed overnight, and the Church would not readjust to a new liturgical spirit and program without a grinding of the gears that would become almost ear-shattering. So, we shall see, this came to be largely a pyrrhic victory, and the results have tended to be as frustrating to the advocates of liturgical renewal as to their adversaries. Indeed, some of the vicissitudes of the Church's liturgical life of late have been no less exasperating to liturgists than the limitations which obtained before the Council, and it is becoming quite clear that our reform of the liturgy has exposed as many problems as it attempted to solve.

CHAPTER THREE

The Advent of Renewal
Vatican II and Beyond (1964-1970)

T HE ANXIETY OF many for liturgical reform, in the years
just before Vatican II, was not merely a concern with
the external niceties of ecclesiastical rituals. To some degree
the liturgical movement, at least in the United States, took on
the dimensions of a revolt of taste, an uprising against the
mundane boorishness of myriad aspects, not the least of
which were manifested liturgically, of the American Catholic
experience—a rejection of the typically pusillanimous views
and folkways of a significant proportion of American
Catholics.[1] This meant a certain tendency for those who
favored *aggiornamento* in liturgy to yearn for it in other
spheres as well. Those who detested the saccharine renditions of *To Jesus' Heart All Burning* at the Offertory during
"low Mass" were prone to be sick and tired of the Legion
of Decency pledge; those who advocated a vernacular Mass
with congregational participation were likely to be in
sympathy with the theological ventures of John Courtney
Murray and Gustave Weigel;[2] priests who wore conical
chasubles or had enamel-covered chalices (especially in
bright colors or with unusual designs) were probably sub-
scribers to *Commonweal, The Critic* or maybe even *Jubilee*

---

1. Cf. Garry Wills, "A Farewell (Quite Fond) to the Catholic Liberal",
   The Critic 29:3 (January-February, 1971), pp. 14-22. Wills does a
   rather clever job of describing various facets of Catholic progressivism
   as it flourished in the fifties and the early sixties. One of his theses,
   which I agree with, is that the "movement" was to a large extent a
   revolt in matters of taste.
2. Ibid. Cf., **Transformation in Christ**, chap. 3.

[39]

and *The Catholic Worker,* to say nothing of *Worship.*[3]

To a large extent, identification with the liturgical movement, as it was generally called, became a status symbol, either positive or negative. To its detractors, membership in "the movement" identified one as impractical, out of touch with reality, insubordinate, snobbish, irreverent, an "egghead", or even (in the case of males) effeminate. Within "the movement", membership in the ranks of the *cognoscenti* was a rare privilege, signifying unusual sensitivity, breeding, good taste, awareness, erudition, piety, vision—and the antithesis of everything about the Church (particularly the hyphenated-American Church of the immigrants) that was crude, stupid, backward and reeked of the ghetto. In a word, a host of battles—theological, sociological, cultural, economic, political—came to be fought on the liturgical turf.

Those who took seriously the liturgists' teachings about the social nature of the sacraments, principally the Eucharist, were generally readers, quoters of and tub-thumpers for the social encyclicals. Liturgical liberals were usually political liberals, and those who belonged to the Vernacular Society or the Pius XII Society were probably also members of the Catholic Interracial Council or the Young Christian Workers.

So it was that a new vision of the Church's ritual became intertwined with a new vision of the Church itself. The old vision of the Church was one of episcopal and sacerdotal autocracy, with little or no accountability to the passive, docile laity. Thus it was entirely appropriate that Mass should be "said" by the celebrant in the mutterings of a

3. Ibid. It is worth noting that those who exhibited deviations from the norm of the American Catholic experience in those days were highly suspect, even though they usually never deviated from authentically Roman Catholic faith and practice. Witness the example of the Jesuit priest I knew whose superiors criticized him for preaching a sermon on the doctrine of the Mystical Body, as it was treated by Pope Pius XII in his 1943 encyclical **Mystici Corporis Christi.** Cf. Chapter 2, **supra.**

foreign tongue, with his back to the congregation. It was wholly in line with the idea of "the clergy prays; the laity pays"; completely consonant with the idea that "Church" was to be equated with "clergy".[4] But those who held the opposite views liturgically—whether they knew it or not— were campaigning for far more than rubrical adjustments. When they demanded that their priests turn around and face them, and speak to and with them in a clear voice and in their own language, they were stating their case for a Church which was less vertical than horizontal, less *gesellschaft* than *gemeinschaft*,[5] less superstructure than community. Whether it was known then or not, the agitation for a vernacular Mass *coram populo*, complete with lay lector or commentator, was a preface to later demands for the opening of the Church's financial records, the invasion of the theological profession by the laity, or the insistence that married clergy exercise the ministry alongside celibates. One can only speculate as to how much of this was grasped, even subconsciously, as recently as the very early 1960s. But it now helps us to understand the passion with which the battles concerning liturgical reform were waged. Those who feared change in the more serious matters felt that there was naught to be gained, indeed, much to be lost—in allowing the slightest chink in the armor of the triumphalistic Church

---

4. Catholics, of course, have no patent on such an unhappy equation. Cf. this preface to a memoir of a nineteenth-century Episcopal cleric in England: "'Twenty Years in the Church!' But are not the Laity members of the Church as well as the Clergy? I reply, that the precise expression, 'being in the Church,' is universally understood of the Clergy alone."—James Pycroft, **Twenty Years in the Church** (London: L. Booth, 1859), p. v.

5. **Gemeinschaft** denotes a social orientation which is essentially personal and communal; **gesellschaft** one which is essentially objective or organizational. Cf. Andrew M. Greeley, **The Hesitant Pilgrim** (New York: Sheed & Ward, 1966) and **Transformation in Christ**, Chapter 5, especially pp. 104-112.

[41]

of the late nineteenth century. Those who hoped, even in the unexplored recesses of their psyches, for more serious reforms in the Church, saw the visible, external—sometimes almost superficial—facets of the Church's liturgy as a good place to begin.

Some of the great emphasis on issues liturgical, in the pre-Conciliar era (especially just prior to the Council) was because of the centrality of the sacraments in the Catholic *weltanschauung* of the time, and the abiding belief that the more vexatious problems of Catholic existence did not admit of change nearly so readily as did the liturgy.

The period after World War II was one in which Catholic theological scholarship and publication, eventually on the popular levels, tended to rediscover the Biblical *kerygma* which zeroed in on the saving power of Jesus' resurrection, and the dynamic power of the risen Christ present in all of the sacraments, most especially the Eucharist. Theologians were intently listened to, and often enthusiastically cheered, when they taught that Jesus in the glory of his resurrection encountered us sacramentally in such wise as to transform us inwardly, thus rendering us fit and effective cooperators with him in the renewing of the world. On a cruder level of expression, it became commonly believed that the sacramental liturgy was the fuel for the civil-rights movement, the Alliance for Progress, the Peace Corps, the ecumenical movement, and the Teilhardian convergence of all mankind in a finally successful drive to rid the world forever of alienation, injustice, strife and war. If one was to change the world, it seemed eminently sensible to begin by changing the liturgy.

And those who loved the Church, but were impatient with it, saw the liturgical arena as the only place where they might foresee a meaningful contest, let alone a victory of any sort. The various elements of the Catholic milieu that militated against ecumenical progress could not be dealt with so long as we kept an unreformed liturgy. Moreover, the more aggravating internal problems of the Catholic community (e.g., the contraception issue, or the question of priestly celibacy) were so generally acknowledged as closed issues that there was no apparent sense in attacking them. For any reformer, the liturgical intransigents would be formidable enough as obstacles. Yet perhaps a few felt that, if careful historical and theological scholarship could have its day in court, so as to occasion re-examination of the liturgy, perhaps it could eventually do likewise when it came to the more deeply-seated controversies that gnawed at the Church from within. In this connection, it might not be inappropriate to suggest that the liturgical scholarship of men like Josef Andreas Jungmann was running interference for the studies on the relationship of priesthood to celibacy done by men like Ruud J. Bunnik, or those on contraception done by John T. Noonan, Louis Janssens, Franz Böckle, et al . . . or even the study on infallibility published by Hans Küng.[6]

For good or for ill, the advocates of liturgical reform in the Roman Church came to be associated with all that waited in the wings during the Second Vatican Council. To some liturgists, this was a gratuitous compliment; to others, a gratuitous slur (depending, of course, on one's standpoint). Considering the intensity which characterized so many intramural disputes within the Church in the 1960s, it is not difficult to imagine how the reformation of the liturgy— in itself not a central issue—became a most important arena.

6. Cf. Ruud J. Bunnik, "The Question of Married Priests", **Cross Currents** (Fall 1965—Winter 1966); John T. Noonan, **Contraception** (Cambridge: Harvard Belknap Press, 1967); Franz Böckle, ed., **Moral Problems and Christian Personalism**, Volume 5 of **Concilium** (Glen Rock, N.J.: Paulist Press, 1965); Hans Küng, **Infallibility? An Inquiry** (Garden City, N.Y.: Doubleday & Co., Inc., 1971).

On the other hand, Council *periti* preparing for the sessions at the Vatican saw the liturgical *schema* as one of the less controversial items on the Council agenda. One such *peritus* told me, before the first session of the Council had even opened, that many Bishops there would find the pastoral motivations and implications of the liturgical *schema* unobjectionable; furthermore, he opined, many of the Council Fathers would be ready to endorse liturgical renovations that might have been less than fully pleasing to them personally, so as to render more credible some questions or objections—even final votes of *non placet* or *placet juxta modum*—which they might have to express in other areas.[7]

Acceptance of the *schema* on the liturgical renewal at Vatican II was almost a foregone conclusion. Between sessions, Archbishop John Krol of Philadelphia told visitors at the 1963 North American Liturgical Week that the Council Fathers had accepted "the bilinguality of the Latin liturgy".[8] If this seemed a piddling admission, it was a giant step from the year before, when representatives of the Vernacular Society—who were heroes at the 1963 Philadelphia Week— were prohibited from meeting in conjunction with the 1962 Liturgical Week in Seattle.[9] As Archbishop Krol and others observed, the reform of the liturgy was impending not for its own sake, externally, but for an internal reason, the

---

7. **Placet** was the Latin term used to signify a positive or approving vote; **non placet** was the reverse; **placet juxta modum** signified acceptance with reservations. For an interesting description of the internal procedures of the Council cf. Robert Blair Kaiser, **Pope, Council and World** (New York: MacMillan, 1963).
8. Cf. The Renewal of Christian Education (Proceedings of the North American Liturgical Week, Philadelphia: The Liturgical Conference, 1963), p. 57.
9. The Vernacular Society was denied a meeting room on the premises at Seattle, since "Week" officials did not want to antagonize the hierarchy. Cf. **Transformation in Christ**, p. 113, fn. 7.

facilitating of congregational involvement—spiritual above all—in the liturgy, especially the Eucharist.

It was for this reason that the liturgical *schema* took the shape that it did, citing the participation of the congregation in the liturgy as the end to be sought above all, and subjugating the fine points of liturgical renewal to the achievement of that end.[10] For the same reason (as well as for the sake of an initial compromise), the first renovations of the liturgy would be envisioned as macaronic, i.e., alternating in language between the traditional Latin and the vernacular of each locality in question.[11]

On December 4, 1963, the actual promulgation of the Constitution on the Sacred Liturgy *(Sacrosanctum Concilium)*[12] took place at the Vatican Council, its practical implementation to take place on the First Sunday of Advent in the following year for the United States. For advocates and adversaries alike, the other shoe had dropped. A vernacularized, congregationally-participated liturgy was now on record as the clear will of the Church at its highest level of authority, the Pope in concert with the College of Bishops in Council. The specific guidelines in the Constitution, and subsequent instructions, would mandate certain elements of reform far more forcefully than had the "September

10. Cf. The Dogmatic Constitution on the Sacred Liturgy (**Sacrosanctum Concilium**) in Walter M. Abbott, ed., **The Documents of Vatican II** (New York: America Press, Association Press and Guild Press, 1966), #s 1-14. Section numbers cited refer to those within the particular document in question, regardless of cloth or paper edition of Abbott and their various systems of pagination.
11. Ibid., #s 15ff. Also Cf. **Pius XII Newsletter** (Chicago, Ill.), October, 1963, December, 1963, February, 1964, and my analysis of "Vatican II and Liturgical Reform", **Christian Art**, April, 1964. In the latter article, I reflect the expectation of a June, 1964, implementation for **Sacrosanctum Concilium** in the U.S.; it was eventually moved back to the First Sunday in Advent, that year.
12. Ibid.

Instruction" of 1958, and would appear as a vindication to liturgical reformers and a paternal admonition to those who would frustrate them.

But, as we are all painfully aware, the liturgical renewal ushered in by Vatican Council II did not deliver all it promised, perhaps not even most of what it promised. Throughout this country and others, there were parishes and even whole dioceses which were thoroughly unprepared for the changes in the form of worship when they were to be put into effect. Celebrants, musicians, pastors, parishioners, the new "lectors" and "commentators" in many places were bewildered, not aided, by a series of alterations which they were hard put to understand or implement. In many instances, even sincere and conscientious following of the instructions left much to be desired, if not in the execution of the forms, then surely in the response of the worshipping community. This was so in 1964 and 1965. And today, about a decade later, we are hardly in a position to assert that the situation has improved dramatically. In all too many cases, the reform of the liturgy has been little more than an unmasking of its problems, and a rather discouraging mandate to rectify more problems than we thought could ever be there in the first place. What are some of the reasons for this? At least the following are key factors:

1. *Expecting too much from vernacularization.*

As a student in high school and college, I and some of my contemporaries became quite attracted to the Byzantine Rite celebrated at the Jesuits' Russian Catholic Center of Our Lady of Fatima in San Francisco. Obviously, a key facet of this appeal was the fact that the Oriental rites utilized vernacular languages in the liturgical celebrations, or in our case English.[13] I can remember, one morning after the Divine

13. Cf. **Transformation in Christ**, pp. 93-94.

Liturgy, expressing to the priest at the Center my admiration for his rite and my impatience with our own (the Council was yet to convene). Father replied by telling me that the Byzantine Rite had more problems than the Roman Rite in its attempt to be a viable avenue of worship for the Catholic community, but that I had become distracted by the superficial question of language. Wait until you have gotten *your* liturgy in the vernacular, he told me, and you will see that you still have many liturgical problems to be solved.[14]

Vernacularization of the Roman Liturgy exposed the redundant nature of so many of our Proper *schemata* in the sanctoral cycle of liturgical feasts, the inadequacies in our cycle of Scriptural readings for Mass, the inappropriateness of some of our Sequence chants (most obviously *Dies Irae*). It solved none of these problems, in itself, although it did call our attention to them so that each one in turn could be (and was) treated. Furthermore, vernacularization in itself could hardly solve a number of problems pertinent to the worship life of the Church which were about to surface during the 1960s in any event: the religious crisis in human lives brought about by the turbulent events of that "decade of disillusionment", the alienation of so many young people from their traditional worshipping communities, crises of belief and practice in individual and social morality, the opening of painful questions about the relationships between Church institution and individual, sacred and secular, clergy and laity, authority and conscience . . . each one of them bound to come to the fore during the years just after the Council whether or not there had been a Council or a reform of the liturgy, but the Council and the reform only made too many of us hope that we "had the problems licked" when in fact we didn't and indeed couldn't have them licked.

14. Ibid. The priest in question was Father Karl Patzelt, S.J.

2. *Inadequate preparation of the Catholic community for change.*

The Constitution on the Sacred Liturgy makes it clear that the implementation of its reforms would have to be predicated on thorough instruction of the clergy and laity in preparation for the new liturgical life of the Church.[15] There are examples of places where this went on even before the Council opened (e.g., the Archdiocese of Seattle under Archbishop Connolly had an extensive liturgical-education program by 1962). But there are too many examples of places where almost nothing was done to prepare the laity or clergy for intelligent participation in a new liturgical format. And there are also some examples of "preparation" so inadequate as to be ludicrous. Witness this announcement made on the last Sunday after Pentecost, 1964, from the pulpit of a New Jersey parish known for its "openness" to new liturgical ideas:

> "As you probably are aware, there will begin next Sunday the implementation of a series of changes in the Mass issued by the Holy See from the Second Vatican Council. Some parts of the Mass will now be in English, and you will be expected to join in some prayers and responses with the priest; texts will be provided for this purpose. Also, you will be asked to join in the singing of hymns, some of which are familiar to you and some of which are new; texts will be provided for this purpose also, and there will be a brief practice before Mass. We realize that this will be difficult for many of you, but realize that this is the will of the Holy Father, the Vatican Council and His Excellency, and we know we can count on your fine cooperation just as we have so many times in the past."[16]

This was in one of the "best" parishes in the State in terms of

15. Cf. Abbott, op. cit., #s 1-12.
16. This is slightly—but not significantly—paraphrased. The name of the parish is omitted in light of the fact that no purpose would be served by compounding ineptitude with embarrassment in this instance, especially in what is still one of the "better" New Jersey parishes liturgically.

liturgical preparedness. The preparation of the clergy in that diocese was not much better: a single study day was devoted to explaining the rubrical changes to the priests; this left virtually no time to treat anything beyond the mere mechanics.

The sort of "preparation" afforded the clergy and laity in most places presumed that the liturgical readjustments of 1964—unprecedented in the history of the Church—would require little more "briefing" than directions to a Knights of Columbus communion-breakfast. Indeed, in the parish example cited earlier, the announcement of this historic change came sandwiched between two routine parish announcements (one of them, I recall, had to do with a Holy Name Society meeting). This type of "preparation" was in a way consonant with the mythical stereotype of the Church as a monolith and all its members as sheep. The announcers of liturgical change in 1964 didn't realize that the changes in question—in most cases—did not have the sort of gradual introduction which would have come with implementation of Pius XII's encyclicals and the "September Instruction", and that these changes provided a classic illustration in the concrete order of the Biblical image about trying to pour new wine into old wineskins. If the individuals who were responsible for the heralding of liturgical *aggiornamento* in 1964 had been employed on Madison Avenue trying to induce the public to accept a new type of soft drink, they would all soon have been out of work.

The leaders of the grass-roots Church in 1964 had no appreciation for the profound nature of the changes they were visiting on their people; if they had, they would have embarked on a long, thorough program of acclimation for them, carefully balancing the changes with indications of stability in the Catholic subculture, adroitly juxtaposing new information and technique with the solidifying of things already known or learned, continually making the average Catholic feel in his heart of hearts that what was coming represented more opportunity than threat.

But it was not done. No planning, no real explanation, no subtle appreciation for the psychology of the thing. Just as in the days before Vatican II, the liturgy was left to "take care of itself" once the requirements of rubrics and Canon Law had been fulfilled. The result, in too many cases, was a liturgical experience which fit the People of God no better than the Roman Mass of old, and perhaps less well, simply because of its awkward newness.

3. *The monastic character of the liturgical movement.*

The monastic atmosphere that pervaded the liturgical movement in the twentieth century brought to that movement many benefits such as scholarship and a certain emphasis on aesthetics.[17] It brought with it some disadvantages as well, not the least of which was the theoretical top-heaviness of many of the liturgical reforms. Too many of the finer points of the liturgical renewal, it now comes clear in retrospect, were proposed by liturgical experts for liturgical experts, but often did not fit the actual situation of the people (including the parish clergy) who were unable to either understand or implement some of these things. Though this would have cut them to the quick, the scholars and professors and monks should have taken into account the fact that—even after the momentous events of the Council—many of the parochial clergy and most of their parishioners would not read *The Documents of Vatican II,* any of the liturgical instructions or communications of the Pacelli pontificate, any of the prevalent liturgical literature like *Worship, Christian Art, Pius XII Newsletter* or *Liturgical*

17. Cf. chap. 2, supra.

Arts, or even some general periodicals like *America, The Clergy Review, Commonweal, Jubilee* or *The National Catholic Reporter.* In a word, the practically-oriented grass-roots Catholics of the United States would not be steeped in the theory behind the liturgical reforms and would not immediately recognize the reasons for singing at Communion, having the altar face the people, or having the congregation sing "Old Hundredth"[18] as a recessional hymn.

Not being familiar with the fact that the Communion antiphon in the Mass is a shortened version of a Psalm-and-antiphon chant, most of the grass-roots Catholics would view singing at Communion time as a bizarre distraction; unaware of the venerable practice implied in the *omnium circumstantium* of the Roman Canon, they would view the *versus populum* altar as some irreverent audio-visual stunt; not prepared for the fact that vernacular hymns common to Christian traditions could be appropriate for Eucharistic worship, they tended to view the "bringing in of Protestant hymns" as something that had been exacted from the Church as a concession in a very suspicious ecumenical movement ("Isn't that what that Council was about—all that ecumenical stuff?")

In addition, too many of the monastics who laid plans for the restoration of the Roman Liturgy did too much of their planning and dreaming in places where the liturgy could be celebrated under practically ideal conditions: voluntary congregations eager to enter into communal celebration of the rites; congregations schooled in the music of the liturgy; musicians capable of the best performances;

18. Often referred to as "Praise God from Whom All Blessings Flow" or "From All that Dwell Below the Skies" (Louis Bourgeois, 1551, alt.). The Doxology is commonly attributed to Thomas Ken, 1709, and the first portion, "From All That Dwell. . . ." to Isaac Watts, 1674-1748.

aesthetically and architecturally perfect places for liturgical celebration (one thinks here of the chapel at St. John's Abbey, but there are other examples); celebrants determined to bring their best to the worship-action of the community. Too few of them contemplated what would happen if the liturgy were put into a church building that was almost impossible, or introduced to a congregation totally unready for this sort of thing, or a celebrant equally unready; too few of the musical experts planned for the transmission of their ideals into the hands of the nice but inept lady down the street from the church who would play the organ for practically nothing and be worth her wages.

In addition (as we noted in the previous chapter) too many of the monks were removed from direct influence in the Catholic community at large; their membership in religious orders precluded them from positions of pastoral leadership, and they were able only to theorize, to recommend, to lecture, to plan, to stand by and hope while others were charged with the responsibilities of carrying out the reform which the monastics had articulated. (In the context of "monastics" here, I refer not only to obvious examples like the Benedictines, but also to less obvious ones like the Jesuits, whose influence was largely confined to their work as professors and authors.) These monastics were to learn, often most painfully, that what made perfect liturgical sense in the pages of liturgical periodicals or in the abbey chapels did not translate perfectly—or sometimes very well—into the parishes of Milwaukee, Brooklyn and Oakland.

One of the chief factors here was the failure of many liturgists to realize that while the post-Conciliar Church ratified their theological insights concerning the liturgy, and vindicated their persistent arguments for specific reforms (chiefly introduction of the vernacular, but others as well, e.g., Mass *coram populo*), the Church could not and would

not legislate *taste*. In the pre-Conciliar stages of liturgical
renewal in this century, the Church had been less than fully
successful (to say the least!) in eradicating maudlin liturgical music and replacing it with Gregorian chant or the
better traditional and modern music of the Church; likewise,
the many principles enunciated concerning proper liturgical
art and architecture did not always make the leap from the
pages of ecclesiastical documents to the brick and mortar
of church facilities. These liturgists should have realized
that the triumph of their viewpoint in the forum of the
Council would not rub out everything that was inadequate
in the liturgical attitudes and tastes of the Church as a
whole. But this many did not realize. One reason, perhaps, is
that they had encountered so much opposition and ostracism
in the years just before Vatican II that they were forced
to turn in on themselves, to adopt an attitude of "just you
wait until the Council", to let their imaginations run amok
in predicting the turnabout that was sure to come in that
"Day of Yahweh".

As I observe in my previous volume *Transformation in
Christ:*

> For those like myself who have been involved in the liturgical
> renewal of the Church for some years, there has been a certain
> amount of unpopularity in Catholic circles. In recent years, we
> have been blamed at every level (parish, diocese or wherever we
> have worked) for change having come too quickly or too slowly,
> too radically or not seriously enough, and so on. A decade ago, it
> was worse, and we were not only looked upon with some disfavor,
> but also with genuine curiosity, if not downright incredulity. In
> those days, the bias was all one-sided, though. **A liturgical left-
> wing had not really developed in the Church, only a right-wing
> which kept insisting that we, following the encyclicals and instruc-
> tions of the Popes, were the left-wing!** (emphasis added)[19]

In such an atmosphere, it was not at all difficult or un-

19. **Transformation in Christ**, p. 93.

likely that frustration on the part of liturgical "movers" would become expressed in clannishness, and even a certain sort of gnosticism.[20] The liturgical movement began to degenerate into a movement of *taste*. Any person sincerely and steadfastly dedicated to the renewal of the liturgical life of the Church would bristle at that very suggestion. Indeed, it was often enough insisted by critics of the "movement" that what was involved amounted to nothing more than a matter of taste or individual preference, and how the liturgist would consider that a theological calumny! Yet an undue insistence on some peripheral aspects of the liturgical renewal—occasioned by frustration and ostracism—no doubt put many liturgists in the position of lending credibility to their very adversaries in the Church in those days. Thus, too many sensitive and sincere advocates of liturgical renewal failed to realize that the Council would not exorcise from the Church all that was mediocre, maudlin, mass-produced, offensive to the *cognoscenti*. They did not realize that the tastes of most Catholics, and their abilities for expression of their tastes, would remain essentially similar after the Council to what they had been before, that their views of the Church as institution would not turn around overnight, that their notions about the role of the laity in the Mass—building up over centuries, let alone decades—would not go out of existence upon issuance of an ecclesiastical ukase. The Church after the Council, as before, would be made up of the same parishioners, the same pastors, the same bishops coming home from the Vatican, the same musicians and architects and publishers and superiors and religious. We would be the same Church as before, only perhaps a bit more defensive in the face of impending change which was not adequately understood. This realization, had it come

20. To which I plead guilty; loc. cit.

earlier, might have taken the edge off of some of the victory celebrations that took place after the promulgation of *Sacrosantcum Concilium* in December of 1963, but would also have alerted liturgists more fully to the disappointments and responsibilities they would have to face in the advent of the liturgical reforms of November, 1964.

4. *Reluctance or inability to implement liturgical changes.*

We noted above that the Church after the decrees of the Council would necessarily be the same Church, only a bit more defensive in the face of renovation. The Church, as total community, was also unprepared for the sort of change that was to come with the liturgical reforms of Vatican II. Most Catholics, even into the early 1960s, had been brought up in a piety which demanded silence in Church, separation between laity and altar, and Latin in the Mass. These elements were by no means essential and unchanging, but many Catholics did not know that, and were unable to see the differences between such tangential earmarks of their faith and the more essential elements of Catholic belief and practice.[21] So it was that many Catholics who heard of the coming liturgical renovations began to view them as an ecumenical gesture of dubious worth, something to "make the Church more Protestant", never realizing that these restorations to the authentic spirit and observance of the liturgy were intended to render the Church more truly Catholic.

Many who did not view these changes as downright heretical or dangerous[22] tended to see them as at best super-

---

21. Ibid., Chapters 1 and 2; also cf. my introductory essay "Changes" in **To Be A Man**, Proceedings of the College Theology Society, ed. George Devine (Englewood Cliffs, N.J.: Prentice-Hall, Inc., 1969), p. 6.
22. Cf. Dietrich von Hildebrand, **Trojan Horse in the City of God** (Chi-

fluous. These were the Catholics who had been brought up, theologically, on a misunderstood notion of *ex opere operato* (whether or not recognized in those terms).[23] The Council of Trent, defending the traditional Catholic doctrine of sacramental efficacy, insisted that the sacraments were effective avenues of grace for their recipients and for the Church as a whole even in the case of a sacramental minister who was personally unworthy; in the technical language of the Conciliar decree, the sacraments were valid and efficacious not *ex opere operantis* (by virtue of the person performing the work) but *ex opere operato* (by virtue of the work being performed).[24] An understanding of this theological utterance in its context makes clear what the Council meant: Christ in his Church is sacramentally present in such a dynamic fashion as not to be thwarted by the unworthiness or sinfulness of any particular human minister of a sacrament. But over the centuries between Trent and Vatican II, *ex opere operato* became misinterpreted in the folk-Catholic scheme of things to mean that as long as the minimal elements of sacramental validity (proper matter and form) were satisfied, nothing else was needed. This misguided reverence for the sacramental presence of the Lord came dangerously close to a sort of magical superstition. And those who followed it—however sincerely—tended to believe that the graces they enjoyed through the sacraments could not be enhanced by liturgical renewal any more than they could be diminished by an unworthy minister. Thus, to this way of thinking, any sort of liturgical change would have amounted to "so much extra work for nothing": in this context, liturgical

cago: Franciscan Herald Press, 1967).

---

23. DS 1608, 3844.
24. Loc. cit.

aggiornamento would have been inefficient. This attitude was well summed up by a pastor in Newark who in the Fall of 1964 attended a priests' study day in his Archdiocese to explore the impending liturgical changes. After lectures, demonstrations and the like, a question period took place, where the pastor asked the speaker: "All I want to know, Father, is *how much of this stuff do I absolutely have to put in at my parish?*" (One can imagine the sort of liturgical aridity that has obtained in that parish both before and after Vatican Council II).[25]

Anyone who feared the liturgical changes as an ecclesiastical sell-out, or dismissed them as so much useless fol-de-rol, would not do any more than was demanded of him by the Church as a matter of obedience. In many a parish (even throughout some dioceses where the bishop thought this way, regardless of any *placet* he might have recorded at the Council) this meant that the vernacular was introduced into the Mass, but the prayers were mumbled as hurriedly in English as they had been in Latin; there was no attempt to lead the congregation in their responses, let alone involve them in any sort of processions or hymns. Furthermore, the congregation might be provided no materials with which to follow the new liturgical texts, and would constantly puzzle at the difference between these and the prayers in their old hand-missals.

In most places, the problems in adjusting to the new order of things liturgically did not stem from hostility or suspicion so much as from confusion and ineptitude. All too often, celebrants were most ill-at-ease trying to adapt to a communal style of celebration when they had been

25. Again, names are being omitted so as to spare unnecessary embarrassment (especially in the case of this misguided but sincere pastor, who has since gone to his eternal reward).

educated and accustomed to a hurried, *sotto voce* reading of the Mass. The introduction of a vernacular Mass, replete with an altar facing the congregation, would take that impersonal, mechanical style of "celebration" (however interiorly devout it may have been) and blow it up larger than life for all to see, and the exhibition was appalling and bewildering.

Church musicians were often less prepared than priests for the "new liturgy". Many of them had been recruited in an age when the function of music in the Church was to provide a devotional background for the ceremonies of the sanctuary. Many of them, too, had only minimal technical competence (in an amazing number of instances, it was presumed that anyone who could play a piano was capable of playing an organ) and their chief attributes were availability and lack of being expensive. Such individuals often had managed to master for themselves (and any choral groups for which they might have been responsible) a limited repertoire involving a couple of psalm-tones for "Propers", a few Gregorian hymns and ordinary-parts, and a smattering of the poorer vernacular hymns that made their way into Catholic hymnals in the late nineteenth and early twentieth centuries. These individuals, in most cases, had yet to readjust fully to the Gregorian revival, let alone more recent trends like the Gelineau psalms or the widening horizons of Catholic hymnody reflected in books like *Our Parish Prays and Sings*[26] or *Peoples Mass Book*.[27] If they had not ventured into a more extensive repertoire in Latin

---

26. Originally published by The Liturgical Press at Collegeville, Minn., in 1956, OPPAS became popular beyond all expectations even before Vatican II; in fact, its revised version did not fare so well after the Council as had the original.
27. Published, and later revised in turn, by World Library of Sacred Music in Cincinnati.

An Agonizing Reappraisal

Mass ordinaries (Goemanne, Woollen, et al, as examples of modern productivity in this area) they continued to demonstrate their limitations—but if they *did* invest time and energy in pursuing more extensive literature in this form, what good would it do in the advent of vernacular liturgy?[28] "New liturgy" made for more music-buying, more music-practicing at a time when most Church musicians' abilities for doing these things was quite limited. Furthermore, the new emphasis on congregational singing in the liturgy tended to make many a choir member or choirmaster feel threatened by liturgical obsolescence: not realizing the complementarity that could and should be obtained between choir and congregation, many parishes disbanded their choirs prematurely, while others "took the side of the choir" in an imaginary conflict between choir members and "ordinary parishioners".

The lay people who were recruited to perform new roles in the services of the post-Conciliar Church were perhaps less prepared for their roles than had anyone been. Unlike priests and musicians and other liturgical functionaries, the lectors and commentators were almost universally newcomers to their positions. The Church had long enjoyed the services of dedicated lay volunteers who would set up chairs, bake cakes, pass the collection basket, sell raffle tickets, sweep auditoriums, run Bingo games, decorate gymnasiums, chaperone dances and ski-weekends, guard children at intersections, campaign for legislative measures that would help the Church or against any that might threaten it, and perform with selfless and unquestioning compliance a host of other chores in the service of the Lord and the Faith. But being lector or commentator was brand new,

28. Cf. my remarks on the piecemeal introduction of vernacular sung Mass, infra.

It meant a transition from silence to vocal participation in church (something previously unheard of for the Catholic layman!) It meant a tremendous reluctance and nervousness on the part of someone who had always been taught to be docile, silent in the Holy Place, and in no way competing with or conflicting with his clerical leaders . . . it smacked too much of "talking back to the priest". It meant, too, making the acquaintance of a whole new series of unfamiliar procedures and terms, in addition to the many strange words in the Biblical texts themselves; there intruded into the Catholic layman's vocabulary such jargon as *ambo*, *lectern* (when did you call an ambo a lectern or a lectern an ambo, and what was the relationship of either to the familiar pulpit?), *commentator* (a poor choice, at least for the English tongue—"Hey, Joe, you commenting at the 12: 15 Sunday?) *lector* (it too took a verbal form, *lectoring*). No wonder the layman cringed at his new role in the liturgy, often looking like a poor soul who had been sucked into his job by the pastor, anxious not to disappoint Father or embarrass himself before his fellow parishioners. One frequently tended to get the impression that saying the responses at Mass was not so much a participation in the renewed liturgy of the universal Catholic Church as it was a favor to the poor fellow who had been placed in the unenviable situation of having to "commentate"[29] at the Mass. One interesting aspect of the whole "commentator" experience in the post-Conciliar liturgy has been the sort of person who has been cultivated in this role. In all too many parishes, the community—often in the person of its clerical leadership—has seemed to turn first to the type of person who had always been willing to do the sorts of chores en-

29. A variant of the verbal form "comment", in American folk-Catholic patois.

umerated above, not considering Paul's dictum that "there are varieties of gifts, but the same Spirit"[30] and the frequent lack of adaptability to this new role on the part of a parish worker accustomed to doing something quite different. This has often resulted in the "lectoring" duties being assigned to people with no background or experience in public speaking, Biblical reading or anything related thereto, who seemed to demonstrate more than their share of stutters, mispronunciations, hesitations, mumbles and other *lapsi linguae* to make the experience traumatic and counter-productive. On the other hand, the professional person in the Catholic parish tended not to be recruited into this type of service, or to be frustrated out of it soon after beginning.[31] In some instances, this seemed perverse "punishment" for lawyers and schoolteachers "too busy to join the Knights of Columbus", in others, an assumption that a willing parish worker (like a curate) could be assigned to do anything that needed doing; in some instances, one cannot help but suspect that the pastor subconsciously recruited the most unseemly specimens of lay representation he could dredge up, so as to perpetuate the myth that only priests were educated and articulate enough to be at home in roles of liturgical leadership of any sort (in which case some laymen would just not be "lay" enough).

In all these dimensions of liturgical performance, it added up too often to an overriding impression that the new wine would indeed be wasted when poured into the old wineskins, and its fermenting would be to no avail. This spillage of the Church's prize liturgical vintage could have been avoided, in large measure, had there been sufficient

---

30. I Cor 12:4-5.
31. The names of prominent American Catholics frustrated out of the job include people like William F. Buckley, Jr., Peter Lind Hayes, et al.

preparation, education, debriefing and rebriefing before the parishes and dioceses were expected to "put in the new liturgy" the way they had in so many instances "put in air conditioning". But such preparation was too often not forthcoming.

5. *Inability of liturgical experts to implement their own proposals.*

We have already acknowledged the advantages and disadvantages that would arise from the monastic roots of the modern liturgical renewal, and as one of the disadvantages we have mentioned the fact that most of the liturgical experts were unable to take direct responsibility for the implementation of their very suggestions. This factor cannot be emphasized strongly enough in attempting to analyze the disappointing results of liturgical renewal in the United States following the decrees of the Second Vatican Council.

In no case related to the instructions and directives of the Council—regarding liturgy, ecclesiology in theory and practice, the life of the Church in religious orders, religious freedom, ecumenism—was it adequately realized that the implementation of these *desiderata* would necessitate a modicum of change in the leadership of the Church in many places and at various levels. This does not mean that the Christian community should have been rent asunder by a series of precipitous and vindictive head-rollings, punitive reassignments or premature retirements; that sort of thing would have gone against human psychology and politics, to say nothing of the charity mandated by the very Gospel, without which renewal would all have been for naught.[32] It *does* mean, though, that the leadership of the Church should at least be expanded sufficiently to allow inclusion in

32. I Cor 13.

the ranks of the very advocates and architects of the reforms heralded by the Vatican Council. It is now a matter of record that this actually took place in far too limited a fashion for the success of these reforms; the area of liturgy provides a prime example.

After the liturgical *periti* had their day at the Council, both they and the Bishops in the *aula* tended to go back home to "business as usual". For the experts in liturgical renewal, this too often meant going back to being tolerated, being ignored, being picked up and used when convenient, and otherwise being dismissed. It was like the experience a friend of mine, a successful author, once had in appearing on a nation-wide TV talk show:

> There you are, famous in front of millions of people, in the limelight, being asked your opinions on all kinds of subjects, hobnobbing with all the celebrities. And when your segment on the program is done, they escort you off stage and there you are, all alone. You go into the washroom and take off your makeup and get on the subway and go home. You are no longer useful to the Beautiful People; it's as if they no longer knew you. And you're still in hock up to your ears, and you wonder if the TV appearance made any difference at all.[33]

For the liturgical *periti,* this meant a brief upswing in the frequency and quality of their being invited to give speeches, write articles, pamphlets or books, teach courses. But in the main, the liturgical-renewal experts were still on the sidelines, not at all able to exercise direct responsibility for or control over the new course they had charted for the Church, all too often compelled to watch their plans carried out by those who did not understand or agree with them. The experience can probably be compared to that of a play-

---

33. The quotation involves slight paraphrasing; the author's name is withheld to spare him embarrassment; he is widely known in American and foreign circles.

wright who sits in the back row of the orchestra watching a director and a cast on stage butcher his every line, and who must read a review that will fault the playwright afterwards for a poor script.

One classic illustration of this sort of thing during the mid-1960s could be found in the "University Churches" operated on some Jesuit campuses around the country. All too often, it seemed, the conduct of the liturgy in these churches was out of the hands of the University professors—especially the theologians—who understood the theory and practice of liturgical reform well enough to teach thousands of students (graduate and undergraduate alike) its fine points. Instead, the liturgy in the so-called collegiate churches usually remained within the purview of the people who had controlled it before, proprietors of a piety and clientele quite foreign to the spirit of the post-World War II Church, determined to preserve "tradition" as it had been understood in the nineteenth century. The theologians who operated alongside such churches were not allowed to trespass, to bring into the churches their insights and understandings for the renewal of the liturgy. As Bernard Cooke once told me in 1964, he would finish a graduate lecture in sacramental theology at Marquette and go downstairs into the Jesuit refectory in Johnston Hall and sit next to the pastor of the Gesu, hoping to engage him in some conversation along the lines of liturgical renewal. All he would talk about, Cooke complained, was baseball. So it was, too, in some other situations, that the mid-1960s found the Jesuit universities teaching liturgical renewal in the classroom but all too often sabotaging it in the sanctuary.[34]

34. The situation eventually improved at least in most of the university churches.

This was partially due to the same phenomenon that was widespread in the American Church at large: the suspicion on the parts of those entrusted with pastoral responsibility that the liturgical experts "didn't really speak for the people" and that the large congregations in these campus churches (largely non-campus people) had to be protected from intrusions of wild schemes into their devotional lives. This meant that the younger and better-educated Jesuits at these universities had to confine to the classrooms their efforts at liturgical education, and watch the practical liturgics of the churches be run by people out of sympathy or out of step with the modern liturgical movement.

Had the theologians and other professors a chance to utilize their university churches as laboratories for the introduction of liturgical renewal in heterogeneous big-city situations, they could have experimented, made some advances and some mistakes, and learned from it all, under the watchful eyes of university sociologists, psychologists, people skilled in the liturgical arts, and the like. Instead, this was an opportunity lost to the American Church, at no small cost to the pace and quality of liturgical *aggiornamento* for large sectors of the Catholic populace in the United States.

The same problem obtained, in many a diocese, between the parishes and the seminaries. Those entrusted with the training of future celebrants of the liturgy were generally unable to influence present parochial congregations. At best, priests teaching in seminaries were "on supply" to say occasional Masses on Sundays in nearby parishes, usually following patterns (some good, some not good at all) set by the local parish staff, usually unable to make significant or lasting contributions.

And diocesan liturgical commissions (likewise sacred music commissions) in too many instances remained what

they had been before Vatican II (perhaps before Pius XII!):
rubrical police forces concerned with preventing violations
of Canon Law and liturgical regulations, seldom leaders of
innovation and creativity who could have encouraged and
assisted genuine liturgical growth, all the while preserving
the necessary obedience to Church authority and laws
that they were charged with. (It is this type of abdication of
responsibility by so many diocesan liturgical commissions,
I believe, that is largely responsible for the sort of liturgical
anarchy that obtains throughout the American Church today.)

In certain special areas of liturgical practice like sacred
music, the same sorry pattern is typical of the American
Church in the middle 1960s (and largely beyond). New
composers who offered to the Church creative ways of
involving the People of God in vernacular worship—like
Dennis Fitzpatrick and Harry Gunther, for example—were
left aside while the official Church busied itself reassuring
the "old guard" in the liturgical music business (e.g., J. S.
Paluch Co. of *Missalette* fame). When we could have been
singing to the Lord a new song, we were listening to Joseph
Murphy's sorry rehash of Gregorian Chant, or Dr. Bennett's
extended *Requiem* for the Gregorian Institute of America.
(Again, I believe, this sort of thing eventually led to nothing
except a lamentable reaction, which took shape in hundreds
of mediocre and downright inappropriate vernacular compositions, or adaptations from non-liturgical sources.)

In all of the above examples, the meaning is clear: without bloodletting, without unnecessary friction being aggravated, the Church could have expanded the ranks of its
leadership to include the planners and practitioners of
liturgical renewal; instead, this was often not done, and the
reformers were separated from their own reforms in a

manner not unlike that of a natural mother having her child
taken away and put into the hands of strange parents. The
result for the Church in this country in the 1960s was a
"liturgical renewal" which was haphazard, awkward, erratic,
confusing—and which, in all too many cases, has yet to
actually begin.

6. *Lack of consistency and economy in introducing*
   change.

We have already dwelt on some examples of how liturgical renovation was introduced with inadequate preparation in most cases, and how this would prove traumatic
for a Catholic people accustomed to stability in their religious
experience. This does not mean to argue for less change
than was indeed necessary, but simply for a more well-
thought-out, well-executed pattern of change than that
which actually supervened upon the American Church in
the 1960s.

Anyone who contemplates seriously and thoroughly the
nature of the Church will come to realize, as Newman did,[35]
its capacity for change in many aspects while remaining
unquestionably and essentially the same Church. This can be
achieved for the Catholic populace only through a pattern of
change which achieves all that needs doing in the name of
renewal while manifesting the abiding continuity of the
Church. As my friend and colleague Bishop John J. Dougherty put it, "Our liturgy must respect the past, while taking
place in the present, with an eye to the future."[36] Needless

35. Cf. my remarks on Newman in Chapter 1, supra; also John Henry
Newman, **An Essay on the Development of Christian Doctrine** (London:
Longmans, Green & Co., 1897).
36. Bishop Dougherty, a member of the International Commission on English in the Liturgy, made this remark at a Mass during which he
preached the homily in 1966. At that time, he was one of the liturgical

to say, there would have to be a balance between those three elements of which he spoke; unfortunately, the liturgical experience was often skewed to the past or future, with the result of an incoherent present.

In a Church where the members of the community of belief were dependent on a stable perception of religious practice, too many changes came too rapidly in too crazy-quilt a fashion; some of the changes did not come quickly enough. There was breakneck speed and foot-dragging in the name of gradualist reform, and the result was almost chaotic.

Vernacularization in itself was probably too gradual. In 1964 we saw the introduction of English in parts of the Mass which "pertained to the people".[37] This was most unhappy a circumstance for all concerned: it left the traditionalists most unhappy since it ended the all-Latin liturgy; it left the vernacularists unhappy as well since it retained so much Latin; it left the theologians unhappy because it perpetuated the idea that some parts of the Mass pertained to the People of God and some did not; it left the liturgists unhappy as well because it implied that their reforms were but audio-visual crutches introduced into certain parts of a liturgy which should really have remained in Latin all along, had it not been for the ineptitude of the laity. This macaronic liturgical situation was remedied after the American Bishops, in 1966, requested, and subsequently received, permission for general vernacularization of Mass, including the central Eucharistic Prayer (Canon). The overriding im-

leaders who did not have direct responsibility for pastoral implementation of renewal, in that he was neither an Ordinary nor a pastor; however, in his capacity as President of Seton Hall University, he lent great support to me and others who worked for liturgical renewal on and near the campus.

37. Sacrosanctum Concilium, #s 14fff.

pression given, however, was one of uncertain compromise, and it may still take the Church some time to recover from that.

A similar situation obtained regarding *Missa Cantata:* vernacular sung Masses came about two years after the initial introduction of English into the liturgy (Easter Sunday, 1966, was a common date for this). This meant, in theory, that the Latin *Missa Cantata* was still the order of the day for a couple of years after the Mass was still vernacularized. It also meant that in practice! Many foot-dragging choirmasters insisted on perpetuating the Latin *Missa Cantata*—even to the point of preparing new settings for it—down to the eleventh hour, when they should have been preparing themselves and their people for a vernacular sung Mass. Once more, the aura of odious and unsure compromise made it difficult for the liturgical renovations to be respectable or credible in the Catholic community at large.

Situations like the above unnecessarily usurped much of the time and energy of the Church during the middle and late 1960s, right up to and including the implementation of Pope Paul VI's new *Ordo Missae* in 1970. All the time the Catholic populace should have been concerned with the interior changes of attitude that were necessary to bring about a new liturgical life for the Church, they were distracted by this or that minor change, in a maddening series of piecemeal adjustments. Many of these adjustments were necessary—at least eventually—but their haphazard patterns of announcement and appearance made for a most confused Catholic community. Pastors were loath to buy new liturgical books, after a while, for fear that they would all become obsolete almost as quickly as they could be delivered. For the same reason, lay people inherently distrusted the various pew-books given them for participation in the ritual (*Parish Mass Book, The English Liturgy Hymnal, We Worship,*

Celebrate!, The Monthly Missalette, Bible and Liturgy Parish Bulletin, revisions of *Peoples Mass Book* and *Our Parish Prays and Sings,* etc.) In like manner, musicians did not feel safe buying or preparing settings, nor did liturgical artists and architects feel safe in making plans that might well be unmade by the next announcement from the Church.

What should have happened, of course, would have been for the Church to introduce at the outset those changes that would have to be made first (vernacular for the whole Mass, in a translation that would be permanent, with appropriate aids for clergy and laity, as well as musicians), then after a time those changes that were less central to the liturgical renewal (changes in the layout of the sanctuary, baptistry, etc., changes in the observance of penitential seasons, the sanctoral and temporal cycles, etc.), taking care at each stage of the process to prepare for each innovation and to measure the response to it before introducing the next. This would no doubt have been agonizingly slow for the liturgical reformers themselves, but would also have afforded them the time to prepare their fellow Catholics for what was coming, in such wise as to make for a smooth transition and not a harsh grinding of gears. Had *this* been begun around 1964, we would certainly be at least as far along as we are now, if not in external changes, then at least in the internal changes of liturgical attitudes and sacramental piety which the whole liturgical movement has been dedicated to promote in the first place.

As it is, about a decade after the promulgation and implementation of *Sacrosanctum Concilium,* and about a half-decade after the implementation of Paul VI's *Ordo Missae,* after all of this external change in our liturgy, there remain a number of substantive questions and problems which we must deal with most seriously.

CHAPTER FOUR

Renewal Found Wanting

THE INADEQUACIES OF THE liturgical reforms that have
taken place since the promulgation of the Constitution
on the Sacred Liturgy of Vatican Council II can be described
as legion, and sometimes as being so genuinely humorous as
to virtually obscure the fact that they are so regrettable. Thus
a series of complaints, condemnations, jokes and wry com-
mentaries have been visited upon the American Catholic
community over the past decade. Unfortunately, many of
these lamentations seem to have generated far more heat than
light. If we are to really seek illumination and not obfus-
cation, we must isolate as best we can the chief areas of
major dissatisfaction with the liturgy in terms of its goal
of fostering the piety and self-awareness of a maturing
Christian worshipping community according to a tradition
and identity which are authentically Catholic. The main
areas to be considered here, in this regard, are: 1) apparent
failure of the liturgical *aggiornamento* to deal adequately
with the dynamics of tension between stability and flexibility; 2) apparent failure to deal with the dynamics of yet
another significant tension, i.e., the tension between immanence and transcendence in religious experience as expressed
in liturgical worship; 3) seeming inability of worship forms
and structures to adapt adequately to different situations
and needs in the existential circumstances in which the
Church today finds itself; 4) a rather obvious tendency of
both its advocates and its critics to ascribe too much significance to the renovation of formal liturgical worship.

1. *The tension between stability and flexibility.*

Margaret Mead, the famous anthropologist, has been quoted many times as saying that anyone born into the world before 1900 was born expecting stability with occasional change, and anyone born after 1900 was born expecting change with occasional stability. Recent experience suggests that this wise observation would be just as valid were its temporal line of demarcation changed to 1950 or even 1960! An anecdote making the rounds of late in New York has it that a little girl was sent by her father to the local grocery store for a quart of milk, but was unable to find her way to the store, so she came back home and reported to her father, "They must have torn it down and put another building in its place!" Unable to find the store, the little girl's first assumption was that, once more, a familiar building had quickly been demolished to make room for a new one. Her father, of course, was inclined to assume that his daughter (who had been to the store probably as recently as a week or so before) had simply lost her way. The father's model or standpoint was one of expecting stability; his young daughter's model or standpoint was one of expecting change. This little story provokes chuckles on the part of most adult listeners, but the chuckles soon give way to the sobering realization that there is, after all, something to this whole business about a "generation gap": all but the very young expect stability, think in terms of it, and are profoundly unsettled if it is not forthcoming.

There are myriad examples of this. How many San Franciscans speak of the "new" St. Ignatius Church (built in 1914)? How many residents of the outer boroughs of New York City still speak of "New York" as in the third person (the boroughs were incorporated in 1898)?[1] How many

1. Cf. the story on the upcoming seventy-fifth anniversary of Greater

An Agonizing Reappraisal

Americans talk of events as being before or after "the War", meaning World War II (which, of course, ended in 1945)? Many New Jerseyans still call the PATH railroad the Hudson and Manhattan (the name was altered in 1962).[2] And when the Duke of Windsor (formerly King Edward VIII) died in 1972, many people around the world were referring to him as the Prince of Wales (since he had travelled around the globe in that capacity in the 1920s). And all because people are generally used to stability, to the way things *were*. Of course, the more ancient the term of reference, the less numerous its repetitors. And now we are seeing the emergence of a new generation which will never consider the rites mandated in 1955 to be the "new" Holy Week liturgy,[3] who will not remember Richard M. Nixon as *Vice* President, who will stare in puzzlement at anyone who mentions Princess Elizabeth, the Pennsylvania Railroad or the Brooklyn Dodgers.

If this is so in life generally, it should prove to be so all the more in the Church, where people have come to expect a great deal of visible stability. Until very recently, the average Catholic has tended to be oblivious to the processes of development in the Church, and has tended to expect minimal change at most. Furthermore, the confusion between substantial and superficial elements in the Church's life in previous religious education and experience has made for a most regrettable misunderstanding of change and even open hostility to it within the past decade. Imagine if you will the innumerable loyal Catholics who had envisioned

New York in **The New York Times**, November 12, 1972, pp. 1f.

2. The new designation stands for Port Authority Trans-Hudson, noting the railroad's takeover by the Port Authority of New York and New Jersey (until 1972 the Port of New York Authority).
3. Cf. my other remarks in this regard as reported in **The Advocate**, November 2, 1972, p. 9.

[73]

Jesus celebrating the Last Supper in Latin, replete with Roman vestments, while the Apostles sang Gregorian Chant.[4] In other words, how many Catholics had come to equate the relatively recent past with "tradition"?[5] The answer, unfortunately, must be far too many indeed. It will at once be supposed that this type of observation obtains in the case of older Catholics, people presently over the age of forty or so. It does, but let us not forget the unsettling effect of change upon the young, including the little girl in the above *exemplum* who thought the store in her neighborhood had been torn down. As I observe in *Transformation in Christ:*

> . . . if the disappearance of the solid, never-changing Church has been a jolt to the oldsters, hasn't it been a boon to the coming younger generations? In all honesty, I don't really think so. This is no criticism of reform in the Church . . . But the Church, having changed in the way that it has—suddenly, without adequate preparation or instruction (despite the warnings of the Popes and the Vatican Council about this), pell-mell, helter-skelter, crazy-quilt, has managed not to shore up its own resources for a new and meaningful encounter with the world, but simply to render itself somewhat incredible as an institution having authority. It is still on record as the Church that doesn't change, but seems preoccupied with seizing every opportunity to do away with jots and tittles . . .
>
> And how can youth view such an institution? Probably in the same light as other authority structures—the family, the school, the government—in which it has tended to lose faith of late . . .
>
> In this regard, even a generation which seems prepared for a Consciousness III world of flux will be hard put to live with the inconsistency of authority structures, the Church included. Indeed, elders may more readily understand or adjust to an authority structure which has to change its procedures owing to unforeseen factors . . . But young people, whatever they may proclaim, seem more dependent on consistency than anyone else, even the very

4. Cf. **Transformation in Christ**, pp. 21ff.
5. Cf. Charles Kohli, "A Time to Be at One", **To Be A Man**, pp. 135-43.

[74]

old. They are perhaps the most intolerant of all generations when it comes to hypocrisy, real or alleged, disorganization, or failure to embody Kierkegaard's notion that "purity of heart is to will one thing".[6]

Today's younger generation, as I have suggested elsewhere, is largely made up of people who ". . . have in many ways had the psychological, emotional and spiritual rug yanked out from under them . . ."[7] And if this be so, then youth is served no better than are their elders by a ". . . Church that doesn't change, but seems preoccupied with seizing every opportunity to do away with jots and tittles whether the case in point be mixed-marriage canons, St. Philomena, Sunday-observance-on-Sunday, women in the sanctuary, St. Christopher, particular or general absolution, host-in-hand communion, Eucharistic Prayers II, III and IV and Penitential Rites A, B and C."[8]

This is not to suggest in any way that the Church should delay change that is necessary, or negate the benefits of changes already in progress. It is to suggest that the Church could make—and still can make—people more responsive to change—intellectually, but more importantly in the psychological and emotional spheres—by introducing change against a background which clearly underscores stability in all matters that are essential. It will often be necessary to do this by leaving alone some matters which are in themselves far from essential, but in which many people have made heavy psychological and emotional investments. Accordingly, in my view, we could have lived for another decade (even another century, if need be) with our Gallicanized Roman Canon and our one-cycle program of Scriptural readings if this would have made the faithful at large more

6. Transformation in Christ, pp. 27-9.
7. To Be A Man, p. 5.
8. Transformation in Christ, loc cit.

receptive to communal participation in a vernacularized liturgy. Likewise, we could have left the Offertory Rite (replete with all its liturgical problems) as it was if this would make people more likely to accept Mass facing the congregation.

The principle I am enunciating here is that in matters liturgical (and in general) there must obtain a certain economy of change, a certain judicious appropriation of the psychological and emotional—as well as intellectual and physical—resources people are able to bring to a situation that demands change, so as to effect those changes which are most needed. This will often mean leaving in abeyance those areas of change which are also desirable, but far less crucial for the time being.

The Church has already lost some opportunities to exercise this economy in change over the past decade. I point this out not in the fashion of one who cries over the spilt milk of history, but to emphasize the fact that the Church in the present and the future—especially in local or "grass roots" situations—still has certain priorities of change and thus many opportunities to achieve those priorities by practicing the economy of change of which I speak.

2. *The tension between immanence and transcendence in worship.*

In 1963, I attended a conference on liturgical music given by the World Library of Sacred Music in Cincinnati, Ohio, with some sessions at nearby Grailville. In retrospect, the experience stands out as an interesting vignette in the recent history of a Church changing and changed. At one of the meetings in the Hotel Sinton, musicians argued over whether a new bilingual *Kyrie* being demonstrated by a composer should be sung in Latin or in English (until one wise man ended the dispute by suggesting Greek!) In another at Grailville, an obscure black priest from Cincinnati (Clarence Rivers, whom many people would go away remembering as "Father Waters") demonstrated the hymn "God Is Love" from what would be published a year later by World Library as his *American Mass Program*. In the middle of it all, Father Eugene Maly, editor of *The Bible Today,* gave an address which lent some theological underpinnings to the considerations of the liturgical musicians in attendance. Concentrating almost exclusively on the literature of the Old Testament, he developed a rather detailed and well-documented dialectic between the image of God as *transcendent* (the One God, like unto Whom there were no others) and the God of Israel as *immanent* (present always to help his people, as with Abraham, Isaac and Jacob). These two elements, Father Maly pointed out, were clearly juxtaposed in the religious experience and expressions of the Old Testament, and should both come through in the religious expressions of those of us who are the spiritual heirs and descendants of the Israelites who worshipped with timbrel and lyre. Fine, Father, fine—a lot of people thought— but what has this really to do with liturgical music? In a time when there is anxiety over the possible vernacularization of the liturgy by the Vatican Council, and thus its possible extent and effect, what need is there for the rehearsal of theological truisms?

Of course, in the few years since Father Maly's address, it has become extremely clear just how important were the considerations he articulated, and how regrettable would be the consequences of ignoring the factors upon which he tried to focus attention. The whole of human religious history, particularly in the Judaic and Christian traditions, involves the tension between man's need for the helping presence of the deity and his understanding that his God is the Other. This has been brought out in the religious poetry

[77]

of the Old Testament, which calls the Lord a shepherd[9] yet is reluctant to utter his holy Name,[10] and surely in the New Testament which incarnates the dialogue between humanity and divinity in the saving person of Jesus the Christ,[11] at once Savior and high priest leading the worshipful response of the saved, simultaneously immanent and transcendent. Any true worship of the God who is Father, Son and Holy Spirit must include both the fact of God's transcendence and also the immanent presence of the Trinity, regardless of whatever external particulars the liturgy may take unto itself.

In even the recent past, the Roman liturgy has been faulted for its excessive other-worldliness, its lack of connection with man's here-and-now experiences and exigencies. This sort of charge was largely correct during times when the Mass was whispered *sotto voce* in a language foreign to the vast majority of the congregation, and celebrated amid a host of symbols which had to be laboriously explained to those who were supposed to perceive their meanings.[12] Indeed, the excessive emphasis on the divine transcendence is responsible for a number of unhappy developments in Catholic liturgical history: the reluctance to allow Holy Communion during "the priest's Mass"; the reluctance to allow the laity to have hand-Missals, the building of altars in the fashion of thrones for the Blessed Sacrament (so as to combat the effects of Christological heresies, we are told), and so forth.[13] Now we are well rid of such things, in the

9. Ps. 22 (23).
10. Cf. Walther Eichrodt, **Theology of the Old Testament** (Philadelphia: Westminster Press, 1961), Vol. I, tr. J. A. Baker, pp. 178-205.
11. Cf. E. Schillebeeckx, **Christ the Sacrament of the Encounter with God** (New York: Sheed & Ward, 1963), tr. C. Ernst, Chapter 1.
12. Cf. Gregory Baum, "Religious Experience and Doctrinal Statement", in George Devine, ed., **New Dimensions in Religious Experience** (Staten Island, N.Y.: Alba House, 1971).
13. Cf. Chapter 1, supra.

wake of a general reform of the Roman liturgy which professed to begin at Trent, tried to begin again in the eighteenth century, and finally took hold in the era of the Second Vatican Council.[14]

Now, if the liturgy lacks a proper balance between immanence and transcendence, it is because of excess in the *other* direction: because our liturgy has become too streamlined, too symbol-free, too pedestrian, too much like the experience of shopping at the local supermarket (not even the folksy delicatessen).[15] As I have suggested, again in *Transformation in Christ*, ". . . in the liturgical renovations of Vatican Council II, the Church managed to adapt itself to the secular spirit of the times as man was about to get sick of the secular spirit of the times."[16] Or as Andrew M. Greeley put it: ". . . the hippies and the Merry Pranksters are putting on vestments and we're taking them off; we have stopped saying the Rosary and they're wearing beads . . . we are making our new low-church liturgy as symbol-free as possible and they are creating their own liturgy which is filled with romantic poetry and symbolism."[17] We are beginning to see a leveling-off of the "hippie" spirit which Greeley characterized at the end of the 1960s, but the problem remains: man who needs symbolic meaning in religious experience has unwittingly reduced his chance of benefiting from it in the liturgy of the Roman Catholic Church in the past decade.

In this regard, there is an obvious danger that too much

14. Ibid.
15. Cf. Dietrich von Hildebrand, **Trojan Horse in the City of God** (Chicago: Franciscan Herald Press, 1967) and Garry Wills, **Bare Ruined Choirs** (Garden City, N.Y.: Doubleday & Co., Inc., 1972).
16. **Transformation in Christ**, p. 21.
17. Andrew M. Greeley, "Dynamic Theology—Today and Tomorrow", in George Devine, ed., **Theology in Revolution** (Staten Island, N.Y.: Alba House, 1970), pp. 26-27.

4

importance could be attached to the very question of vernacularization of the liturgy itself. As C. J. McNaspy and other eminent liturgists have pointed out, a Latin liturgy (often with Gallican accretions and Victorian customs) was more a vehicle for mystification than for a genuine sense of mystery, and it is possible to preserve the latter while doing away with the unnecessary encumbrances of the former.[18] But the Church must deal with the practical dimensions of this, at a time when human beings are beginning to feel that there is not much more personal meaning or identity in their liturgical experiences, and no more feeling of transcendence or of divine presence than in the dispensation of pre-packaged hamburgers at the nearest McDonalds: modern, clean, efficient, somewhat stylized in a contemporary sense, mass-produced, but not personally meaningful. It can be argued, with some accuracy, that some of what used to pass for a sense of personal meaning in religious experience was little more than a superficial atmosphere of ersatz "churchiness", but the fact of its superficiality would argue more for its being replaced by something more substantial than for its being swept away to reveal only a void.

Yet in the process of the liturgical renewal since Vatican II, we have too often replaced one set of mechanics with another, and though the second set of mechanics is designed to serve the needs of the worshipping community in a much more meaningful way than its rather encrusted predecessor, the Church in large measure has failed to make this a reality. The result is often the worst of both worlds: the streamlined, aluminum-and-plastic style of the "new liturgy" combined with the routine, impersonal execution of the old, without any of the old "style" that would serve to cover a multitude of liturgical sins.

18. **America** 109:6 (August 10, 1963).

The transcendent in our liturgy cannot be replaced merely by trying to "go back to the good old days". Those days were surely *old*, but it is hard to demonstrate that they were really all that *good*. We need something far better for the sacramental worship of today's Catholic community. At the same time, we must also remain true to our own culture, our own rite, so there is little to be gained simply by aping the Orientals, whose rich liturgy is their own and not ours. Furthermore, in stressing that the liturgy is the celebration of divine presence in human experience, and not merely the celebration of human aspiration, it will be necessary to reiterate the transcendent dimensions of the liturgy without sacrificing the salutary rediscovery of divine immanence which has characterized our liturgical *aggiornamento* over the past decade and more.

3. *Seeming inability of forms and structures to adapt.*
Over the past five or so years, much has been made of the need to express more flexibility in liturgical forms: why not have a folk-Mass for the youngsters, something for the in-betweens, a special liturgical service for the "golden oldies", and so on? This line of thinking can represent certain truths; it can also lead to certain dangers. One truth it can represent is that flexibility is more endemic to the Catholic liturgy than is uniformity. The uniformity imposed upon the West by Pepin in 754, which has held sway in the Roman Rite until the late 1960s, is familiar to Catholics, but should not be normative for us, as made clear in the various options offered in the *Ordo Missae* of 1970 and subsequent instructions. The danger represented in this type of thinking, though, is that precipitous division within the Church can be aggravated by the dividing of liturgical clusters into categories of age, race, or whatever. We must show all members of the People of God that they are all welcome all

the time at the banquet table of the Lord in worship and celebration, and that no one is disqualified from the liturgical assembly, no one is above or beneath it, simply as a matter of style. At the same time, we should be aware of our own experience in the past decade enough to know that we cannot simply pretend away differences in attitude, preference or orientation in the name of unity; to do that is to ignore a variety of special needs equally, but that is hardly the sort of fairness which we seek in the name of Christ.

Part of the problem has been the tendency to divide existing worshipping congregations into age groups, preference clusters or whatever, so that one physical facility and one parochial staff must be made to serve the needs of more than one type of congregation. For example, this will often result in a "youth Mass" in which the parish *organist* plays "folk hymns" (really!) or a "traditional" liturgy in the environs of contemporary liturgical architecture, even including "pop-art" banners. This type of thing often makes one group feel that its territory is being encroached upon by a band of malcontents in the worshipping community, and oftentimes parochial divisiveness is increased, not laid to rest.

Another part of the problem in this regard is that the average parochial staff member (pastor, curate, deacon, religious educator, musician) is usually unable to deal with a variety of different groups all at once. There are probably a few such people who are able to inspire awe in the rest of us by their carrying-out of Paul's maxim that we be "all things to all men",[19] but to expect that of everyone is frankly unfair to all concerned. I have had occasion to notice what happens in the case of someone who ministers to a group which is essentially homogeneous. He takes unto himself

19. I Cor 9:19-23.

the ways of thinking, feeling and expression which are proper to the community in question. This means (to cite specifics) that some priests I know who have been assigned to work entirely with teenagers have tended to take on teenagers' ways of celebrating, singing, speaking—even though the priest in question might be forty or so years of age. Some others I know have been assigned to work in worshipping communities of much older people, and have taken on *their* ways of looking at things and expressing their experiences and feelings—even though the ministers might be forty years *younger* than the ones they are serving. There is always the danger of this sort of thing being superficial or excessive, but in many instances it is a positive help to the particular community in question in terms of its specific needs. The same observations will obviously hold true for those who minister to groups of Italian immigrants, Chicano farm workers, blind Catholics, Irish-American lawyers, midwestern professors, urban Blacks, New York policemen, Polish teachers, Seattle dockworkers, or what-have-you. But to expect a single minister (again, priest, deacon, teacher, musician) to assimilate within a multiplicity of these communities or sub-communities at once is both unrealistic and unjust. And to impose a multiplicity of worship-forms upon a parochial community which includes a variety of sub-communities might well risk a situation similar to that of the interior decorator who pastes wallpaper over a wall whose plaster is buckling.

In a word, perhaps we need to think seriously about the need for separate worshipping communities with distinct identities to serve special needs, even within the context of existing geographical super-communities. This would have been unworkable some decades ago, when a parish encompassed all the people who could physically reach that particular center for worship and probably no other, but in many parts of the United States this is no longer the case. Even in spread-out suburban communities, the ascendancy of the automobile and the cohesiveness of the nuclear family would make the sort of thing I am proposing both less necessary than in the cities and less difficult than in ages past. But the main thing I have in mind would be the great metropolitan areas, where people live in walking distance of as many a half a dozen Catholic churches, within a public-transit ride of many more, and are often not reducible to the simple quotients of the typically American nuclear family in the suburbs.

Here, where there converge in our super-cities the old, the young, the Black, the single, the widowed, the young new family and the folks whose last has just left home, the "ethnics", the highbrows, the blue-collars, and the buses and subways, there is not the need there was yesteryear for a series of contiguous parochial fortresses with impenetrable geographical perimeters. We already have precedents for the creation of new worshipping communities in our metropolitan areas on the basis of national origin (Italian, Slovenian, Polish, Spanish), specific mission (Chinese, Negro), particular rite (Byzantine, Dominican) or preference of devotion (the "religious churches" of the Jesuits or Franciscans). Perhaps it is time to go a step or so further, in terms of the creation of new worshipping communities and even new ritual categories, so as to meet a variety of needs with a seriously and consciously constructed set of specific ministries. But more of this later in this chapter, pursuant to mention of our next consideration.

4. *A tendency to "expect too much of the liturgy".*

Any list of *lamentabili* must include this. It is by now painfully obvious that both critics of and apologists for the renovation of the liturgy since Vatican Council II have tended to attach far too much significance to the alteration of rubrical details and liturgical forms. A number of us (including the present author) who argued vigorously for the renewal of the liturgy in the late 1950s and early 1960s were often naive enough to believe that the revival of liturgical piety in the Roman Church would be the definitive moment in making straight the way of the Lord, for the ultimate salvation of all mankind through Christ in his Church.[20] We have now come to realize that a renewed ritual, even if perfectly executed, will tend to be a reflection of piety and of solid Christian life at least as often as and probably more often than a cause of it. This does not mean that our efforts at meaningful liturgical celebration should cease or diminish; if anything, the haphazard or halfhearted nature of too many of these attempts in the recent past dictates that we constantly strive for improvement in this regard. However, we must eschew any thought pattern that places liturgy *so* centrally in the scheme of things that other necessary considerations are virtually obscured. A meaningful, tasteful and truly balanced celebration of the sacred mysteries of salvation in the liturgy will necessarily be at the heart of the life of any individual Christian or any worshipping Christian community. But just as the heart does not function without lungs and blood vessels and the like,[21] the liturgy all by itself cannot and should not be expected to fill all the needs of the Christian community or of any individual Christian.

This means that it will never be enough for even the most ardent or expert liturgist to argue and strive for the renewal of the liturgy, period. It will always be necessary

20. Cf. Joseph T. Nolan, **The National Catholic Reporter** 9 (October 27, 1972): 6-7.
21. Cf. I Cor 12:4-31 and **Transformation in Christ,** chap. 5.

to strive for a true revival of internal Christian piety not only in combination with but indeed *in the very context of the liturgy:* as Paul makes clear in I Corinthians 11: 17-34, it is not satisfactory to celebrate the feast of fraternal charity in the name of Jesus unless that fraternal charity has at least a genuine chance of abiding within the celebrating community. Too often in the Church, that fraternal charity does not have that genuine chance, and not necessarily out of ill will—it is quite enough to frustrate the embodiment of *agape*[22] if we have unwieldy structures of organization for our community worship, or ill-advised manners of celebration. And it is even more detrimental to the celebration of fraternal love in a eucharistically-centered Christian liturgy if we do indeed detect within our environment the continuation of social or personal injustices which might be at least minimized by a more conscientious application of the moral principles revealed in the person, the Gospel and the ongoing churchly ministry of Jesus the Christ. There is some evidence, of course, that the Church in itself need not be expected to shoulder every burden of the *saeculum*,[23] but it cannot be denied that the Body of Christ in the world must be careful to incarnate in the world the saving love of the Lord through every possible means. In the first instance, this will mean at least making the Church in itself more truly and visibly reflective of the love that exists between Christ and his members in the world, and that should be manifest among all who aspire to the name of *Christian* as denoting one who loves others.

For most Catholics, the liturgical experience takes place

---

22. The NT Greek word to denote fraternal charity, and also the feast of charity often celebrated in connection with the Eucharist. Cf. Chapter 1, supra, and I Cor 11:17-36.
23. In this accommodated sense, **world** meaning **here-and-now.** Cf. **Transformation in Christ**, chap. 5.

chiefly—if not exclusively—in the parochial structure. The average churchgoing Catholic is one who, every Sunday, or in many places, late Saturday anticipating Sunday, attends a relatively large church known as a parish, his membership in which has been determined by the geographical location of his dwelling. The typical Mass which the parishioner attends is on Sunday, and almost always before about 1:30 p.m., local time. The service lasts about forty-five or fifty minutes, and it is within this period of time that the parishioner hears the Word of God in the Scriptures, prays the responses of the Mass, sings (and sometimes learns) the hymns selected for the Liturgy, contributes to one collection (sometimes more) in support of the Church (principally the parish), is exposed to the announcements of the parish and diocese, and to the sermon or homily. In short, it is within the context of this Sunday parochial experience that the typical adult churchgoer has about ninety per cent of his tangible experience with the Church.

And the experience, in some cases, seems to have been woefully lacking in meaningful and refreshing encounter.

The Mass is now heard in the vernacular. Myriad attempts have been made at developing popular liturgical song, notably in the "folk Mass" category. And a pastor, curate or parishioner may often feel able to boast that "we have the liturgical renewal in our parish", speaking of it as something that was installed in an hour, like a new light fixture.

And that is perhaps the largest part of the problem. In the process of the so-called "liturgical renewal", one set of mechanics has been superseded by another—but it is still a set of mechanics. In liturgy, the dialectical tension that must and does exist between the charismatic or spontaneous and the structured will of necessity resolve itself in the existence of a certain structure that will serve the

[87]

worshipping community. But this is something different: a rehash of the old patterns of decades past, unable to genuinely satisfy the worship-needs of today's People of God, and many of today's People of God—knowingly or half-consciously—feel or reflect the fact.

The attitudes of the past that produced this situation seem to be summed up in terms of Sunday Mass obligation, support of a territorial (sometimes national) parish, and a mass-movement system (no pun intended) that strives for convenience, often convenience for the clergy. Before proceeding further, we would do well to consider these.

The question of Sunday Mass obligation has been debated by learned theologians and high school sophomores, but the official Church has not changed the means of satisfying the obligation or given a new rationale for the same.

I agree very strongly with those who support an ecclesiastical obligation to regular Eucharistic worship for Catholics. To me, the center of the Catholic life is the Mass. This is so when the Mass is celebrated in a group of twelve people around a dining room table, replete with dialogue homily, extemporaneous prayers, folk hymns and the like. It is also so when the Mass is monotonously read (and the word is used advisedly) by a stubborn priest not unlike those described by Graham Greene in *The End of the Affair*,[24] who mumbles with his back to hundreds of anonymous faces in a cold and barren building of horribly negative architectural and aesthetic quality. This is not to say that I am parroting those who have been wont to argue: "The Mass is the Mass, period!" in opposition to any sort of effort at liturgical *aggiornamento*. It is to say that the Risen Lord is present in the eucharistic community of his Church in ways which not only triumph over the temporal/spatial dimensions of

24. New York: Viking Press, 1951.

the human condition, but which come through even despite the failings and inadequacies of his people and even his ministers. Around that banquet table (even if it be a grotesque "soda-fountain" altar that climbs up the back wall of a gaudy 1912 sanctuary), Christ the Messiah is undeniably and salvifically present. If we are his *ecclesia*,[25] we must encounter him there, and with the regularity that has been seen as so important from the time of Paul the Apostle through that of Paul VI.

Be that as it may, though, the post-Conciliar People of God will in fact no longer be satisfied with mere minimal validity. We want sacraments to be just that: to signify what they cause and not only cause what they are somehow *supposed* to signify. And that, of course, is the whole point of the renewal of the liturgy heralded by Vatican II. Furthermore, if the Church of Vatican II can admit that Eucharistic worship is enhanced by vernacular, *versus populum* altars and even guitars, it can certainly admit that the obligation to regular eucharistic worship can be retained, but enhanced by a bit of rethinking and re-emphasis.

Many Catholics tend to think of the Sunday (and holyday) Mass obligation as something that has to be satisfied under pain of mortal sin, period. It is a truism to say that this is a horribly negative orientation. When I began teaching theology to undergraduate collegians in 1964 (before a lot of the present waters had made their journey over the proverbial dam), this seemed to be among their primary religious hang-ups (along with the question of meat on Fridays, which in most cases is no longer a problem of burning existential import). I can remember being asked about this many times (more than nowadays) in the class-

25. Again, from the NT Greek, denoting either the Church as a whole or a particular Church congregation (more literally, worshipping assembly). **Ecclesia** in Latin is a translation of the Greek **ekklesia**.

room, and I felt that I could not answer the question simply in terms of the categories it employed; in fact, I said so.

It had been years, I told them, since I thought of the Sunday Mass obligation in terms of mortal sin. In sincerity, I was speaking for a number of Catholics who had been drawn to Christ present in the liturgy, and who knew the same fact that was at the root of the obligation: The Mass is so centrally the action of the Church that any one who would be a vital member of that Church would in fact participate in that liturgy at least as often as the letter of the law obliged him to, and almost certainly *more* often.

But it can be asked, and quite legitimately, whether that answer takes care of the concern voiced by the original question. Here we have to look at the letter of the law as a reflection or incarnation of the spirit, and (at the risk of appearing simplistic) reply that the well-motivated Catholic who wants to act as a vital member of the Church will practically never absent himself from the community's Mass-action on the principal day of regular worship, viz., Sunday. It will be said, and again legitimately, that this answer leaves numerous circumstances uncovered, e.g., the *occasional* absence of such a person. Assuming no malice, apathy or the like, can we not say that the sincere member of the Church who quite *seldom* misses Sunday Mass, for reasons other than physical infirmity and subsequent confinement, etc., is still a "member in good standing"?

In this connection, I cannot help but remember the Sunday morning of bachelor days when two roommates and I, joined by a couple of friends, spent over half an hour getting one of four cars out of a snow-blocked driveway, so that we could attend a mechanical liturgy in a wealthy suburban parish which could afford $15,000 for new lights in the nave but would not hire an organist or finance other aspects of liturgical renewal. In future years, there were to be other Sunday blizzards. I recall one of these, when my wife and I were part of the throng who had made it through the snow when no other group seemed to, and were herded into a large and cold building for a lacklustre Mass. Both of us had been to Mass at least once during the previous week, and were to do so again during the coming one. We asked ourselves, why not allow the obligation (which we supported) to be fulfilled another day, at perhaps another place of eucharistic assembly? In the sort of weather where nursery school principals and university administrators race each other to put cancellation notices on radio stations, why could the Ordinary not exhort his flock to avoid the hazards and participate in Mass, whenever and wherever possible, during the coming week? That the circumstances justified excusing people from the Sunday obligation may have been obvious to Canon lawyers, but not to most lay Catholics.

Some liturgists have proposed, for some time now, that the Catholic's obligation to join regularly in the eucharistic celebration should be able to take place on any day of the week, and often *not* in the parish as we now know it. It should be at or near one's place of work, on the campus, in the homes of the People of God, in a variety of places "where the action is", facilitating intimacy, informality and genuine personal involvement. But to take this proposal away from the lecture hall or the study and put it into the marketplace, we will have to do something about the structure—particularly financial—of the parish.

According to some, Catholic emphasis on fund-raising and receiving is no less than lamentable; according to all, it is no less than real. Let us not jump into a bloody discussion of whether or not the Church, or Church*men*, always use money in the most efficacious way. The fact of the matter is that this Church, in truth, needs money to carry on the apostolic work of Christ in the world. However, with particular reference to our above considerations, the Church is crippled in a variety of ways by a system which provides that the bulk of the monetary harvest will be reaped in the parishes on Sunday mornings, in ways which range from those of sheepish subtlety to those of the money-changers in the temple.

If we arc to suggest that many Catholics are to exercise their eucharistic membership in Christ apart from the Sunday morning parish experience, we must also say that their support of the Church must take place in another way. If we do not, we are operating outside of the realm of the real world, and many who have genuine and legitimate concern for the exigencies of this real world will give us no hearing.

Let us first think in terms of the New Testament concept of the diocese as coextensive with the *ecclesia,* the "church" that Paul is speaking of when he writes Epistles to different places. It is not long after the Apostolic age when the Bishop often splits his work-load by delegating the duties of the president of the assembly to a priest called a *parokios.*[26] This is how our structural relationship between diocese and parishes begins. Today, funds come into the parishes, and from the parishes into the diocese. Why not reverse the process? In this way, wealthy parishes who have to devise ways in which to use their revenue would be relieved of their problems, and poor parishes might be relieved of theirs as well. Also, the individual Catholic could contribute fairly and regularly to the diocese which (in most cases) takes in both the place where he lives and the place where he works, as well as the place where his children go to grade and high school (and perhaps college). He feels that

---

26. This word obviously gave rise to the English terms parochial, parish, etc.

the financial contribution he makes serves the church nearest his home, the one down the block from his job, the chaplain at his daughter's high school . . . and the parishes in the inner-city ghetto areas for whose apostolate he should and often does feel responsible. He also feels equal membership in the eucharistic community at his own home, that of his neighbor, friend or colleague, or the downtown church.

It is hoped that if this proposal were adopted, donations could be distributed more equitably within a diocesan structure. Instead of monies coming first to the parishes and then to the central treasury of the diocese (by means of assessments, as with the present setup), they would go first to the diocese and then be distributed to parishes according to need. This should prove a boon for inner-city parishes in need of more funds than can be donated by their members. It will probably also seem a catastrophe to those Catholics, lay and clerical alike, who still suffer from the "edifice complex", wherein facilities are obtained whether needed or not, simply to show how prosperous the area is and how successful the parish community is in raising money. It will also enable the layman to donate less frequently, but more fairly. Most laymen today contribute weekly, and what they "put into the box" is often loose change. The proposal at hand would occasion a mail donation, which would prompt the donor to survey his own financial situation and then, with conscious forethought, prepare his offering, usually in the form of a check; this could be done monthly. The psychology here is not unlike that employed in the much-hated "envelope system", except that our proposal does not carry with it the odium of signalling parish membership by handing a man a packet of envelopes and branding him with a number.

Lastly, it should be pointed out that the above suggestion does not preclude regular attendance at a territorial parish, or weekly presentation of one's gift there, as with the present system. It does, however, provide alternatives. And that is precisely what we must do. In a Church where there still exist such truly obscene situations as "seat money" (what was that about money-changers in the temple?), it is clear that the official Church that we know will not give credence to a more flexible view of eucharistic participation without its material exigencies being attended to.

If this is done, the Church's discipline—which presently maintains a Sunday (or vigil) obligation—could eventually be receptive to a more flexible interpretation: attend Mass, in all cases, at least weekly (unless prevented from doing so by some good reason); do this in a large parish assembly on Sunday, if you will; do it around the dining table of your own home, or that of a friend; at work; at school; at the local community center; in a word, participate in the Mass-liturgy of the Church in a way that truly takes into account your identity and your needs. Thus, for a variety of human persons, a variety of liturgical experiences.

Perhaps we should now consider the large parish experience, since it will remain the chief liturgical environment for most Catholics. The present system of several Masses on Sundays and weekdays need not be substantially altered. A number of people will still prefer to join in the liturgy on Sunday morning. But if we remove the idea that all of this must be done before noontime has vanished, and if we eliminate the last vestiges of the belief that people who attend Mass in the evening are lazy, immoral or somehow otherwise suspect, then we also eliminate the "get-'em-in-and-get-'em-out" attitude concerning Mass scheduling. Now there can be more than fifty minutes allotted to a Mass, and more than ten minutes before the next two thousand people swarm in. Afternoon and evening Masses can be offered in abundance on Sundays (in some places, they are still not in vogue, or at least frowned upon). "Not enough time" can no longer be offered as an excuse for the absence of an adequate homily, or other elements of well-done liturgy, or for the failure to rehearse new hymns with the congregation before Mass, or for a hurried-up mechanical celebration of the Mass. And the people who are there need not feel that they are being rushed. They are at home in the house of their Father, and are welcome. They need not fear that devotion will stand in the way of progress. They need not remember the liturgical experience as something squeezed between parking-lot skirmishes.

Now we are ready to begin tailoring our liturgical rite to the needs of the community in question. It would be foolhardy to be too specific in these pages. Laramie, Wyoming and Dumont, New Jersey are different from each other, as are they both from Watts in Los Angeles or Ballard in Seattle. But perhaps some suggestions can be offered that may have relevance to most, if not all, situations.

First of all, in places where this is sociologically and demographically possible, we should be able to think seriously in terms of specifically designed ministries to specific groups and needs, rather than the catch-as-catch-can or "general practitioner" approach that seems excessively prevalent in the parish of today. In a large percentage of cases, oddly enough, this will signal little actual change. Many parochial ministries will continue to be directed at "middle Americans", many communities of senior citizens (e.g., some of our urban apartment areas or retirement communities) will see little or no change of any significance, and collegiate and hospital chaplaincies will operate much as before. The difference, though, would be in the *specifying* of a particular ministry in a special situation, and the conscious development of a staff for such a ministry, rather than the plugging of people into vacancies in the hope that they will then adapt to the exigencies of their new situations —especially if an individual pastoral career encompasses several quite different special situations, as quite a few still do.

More specifically, this would allow for the development of worshipping communities that could direct their resources into the development of liturgy and community witness for youth, for young families with small children, for the elderly, for professional people, and the like. Anyone who thinks this sort of consideration is unnecessary has never been the parent of a two-year-old who finds himself unwelcome at the Sunday morning meeting of the Serutan set, or a senior citizen who feels alienated by the local "teenybopper Mass", or a college professor who is clearly ignored in a liturgical experience directed at a neighborhood in which blue-collar workers predominate.[27]

In a way, this type of pluriform community ministry would be a logical extension in liturgical and ecclesial terms of the ministries already begun in the American Church under such auspices as Young Christian Students, Cana, the Christian Family Movement, various groups of older Catholics, and so on. Only that which takes place in the regular act of community worship would conform more explicitly, and more helpfully, to that which takes place outside of it, in terms of the forms of liturgical experience and expression chosen, and also in terms of the ministry of the Word exercised in the liturgical services.

To facilitate the availability of physical meeting places and celebrating clergy for such ministries, and the adaptability of such liturgical celebrations to the life-styles of those in special need of these ministries, we would insist on the

27. Cf. my article, "Liturgy for Middle-Brows" in U.S. Catholic, May, 1973.

type of flexibility spoken of above with regard to the exercise of the obligation to regular eucharistic worship (as opposed to the obligation to worship each Sunday, or to anticipate Sunday on Saturday). Likewise, we would insist on flexible opportunities for membership in a worshipping community outside the boundaries of what would be one's geographical parish. Indeed, within a densely-populated and highly-churched area (e.g., San Francisco, New York, most other major cities and suburban areas), a number of parishes could combine to share ministry along lines of demarcation which would no longer be geographical, but could now be devised according to various ministries based on different needs. One church could concentrate on serving the many single and widowed people who live in our cities, and who are ignored by family-oriented services; another could minister specifically to teenagers and college students; yet another could deal with the special needs of the 25-to-35 group, the more educated, those more attuned to "traditional" styles of worship, and so forth. Resources for serving these various groups with their special needs would now be consolidated, and no longer dissipated.

The object here would not be to divide the Church. Anyone who has reflected at all on the experience of the Catholic community within the past ten or so years is well aware that we have experienced the pains of excessive division and continued divisiveness already, and that this sort of thing which violates the very nature of Christ's gospel message must be terminated by those who follow his teachings and bear his name. But there is a false "unity" which can be imagined when needs of a special nature are pretended away in the name of "getting it all together". The allocations of resources which I propose would take place along the lines of the type of fences which, as the poet once observed, make good neighbors.

CHAPTER FIVE

Sing to the Lord A New Song

EARLY IN THIS century, the story has it, a Catholic army chaplain in the Philippines sought music for an improvised midnight Mass at Christmas. When nothing else turned up, he procured a local military band. Having exhausted their stock of Christmas carols, by Communion time, they blared forth with a popular march of the day, "Where Do We Go From Here, Boys?" In terms of liturgical music, the question was appropriate then, and it is appropriate today.

Not long before the reported anecdote, Pope St. Pius X[1] had issued his *motu proprio* on liturgical music,[2] and an era of reform and renaissance in the public worship was dawning in the Roman Catholic Church. Seven decades later, the very renewal instituted by Pope Pius himself seems virtually antique in light of the developments which have supervened since Vatican Council II, as far as music for Catholic worship is concerned. While it is clear that forms for worship-music have changed, are changing today and will continue to change in future, it is becoming just as clear that we cannot react judiciously or beneficially to myriad changes in form without serious consideration of principles which should always be taken into account regarding music for worship, its intent, role and execution toward the goal of the most meaningful and efficacious liturgical celebrations we are capable of.

1. Pope St. Pius X is commonly called "the patron saint of the Holy Eucharist" for his efforts at engendering Eucharistic piety among Catholics in the early twentieth century.
2. **Tra le Sollecitudini, ASS** XXXVI (1903): 329-39.

An Agonizing Reappraisal

Here we speak of what I will call *worship-music*. Not only music for worship, but also worship through music, as a most important form of religious expression, which at once involves the worshipper (performer or hearer) intellectually, sensually, physically, psychologically and emotionally, and in such a pervasive way is a major element in the carrying out of Christian liturgical worship.

Worship-music first of all is art. Tolstoi called art an attempt by the artist to convey an experience (in the broad sense of the term) to his audience.[3] With a specifically Christian artist, I suggest that the basic experience (at least implicitly) is of God, whether manifest through his direct invasion of human events as revealed and celebrated in Salvation-History, or in the riches of natural creation,[4] or even in ways which are exceedingly indirect and even—as in the instance of Graham Greene's "tragic sinner" novels—labyrinthine.[5] In Christian art man catches a glimpse of the deity, while expressing a worshipful response; it is—as Romano Guardini noted—". . . essentially a way. The way by which God is announced and presented to man; the way through which man's devotion and love go to God . . ."[6] Music is especially expressive of this type of communication. But, as Suzanne Langer asks, ". . . if we are moved by sympathy, with whom are we sympathizing? Whose feelings do we thus appreciate? The obvious answer is: the musician's. He who produces the music is pouring out the real feelings of his heart. . . ."[7] And here I suggest that worship-music

3. Lev Nickolaevich Tolstoi, **What Is Art?** (London: Oxford University Press, 1932), tr. Aylmer Maude.
4. Brother Justus George, "Idea of a Christian Art", **Thought** 24 (1950).
5. Cf. Anthony West, "Books: Saint's Progress", **The New Yorker** 27 (November 10, 1951), p. 141.
6. Romano Guardini, "Sacred Images and the Invisible God", **Cross Currents** 10 (1960), pp. 11fff.
7. Suzanne Langer, "On Significance in Music" in **Philosophy in a New Key** (Cambridge, Mass.: Harvard University Press, 1942), pp. 113-115.

[99]

will necessarily be different from other types of music; it is unique in that its "composer" and its "audience" are in effect one and the same, viz., *the Church as worshipping community*. The individual Church musician does, of course, compose in his own style, adding his own religious experience or style of expression. Yet while his authorship is in one way his own, his authority (and both words come from the Latin *auctoritas*— the function of giving life, including life in a work of art) comes from the total expression of liturgical worship. An obvious application of this would be the existence of diocesan liturgical music commissions, and in ages past such guides as the Gregorian Society "white list" of approved liturgical music.[8] In a new era of much greater permissiveness in matters liturgical, the acceptance of a community for forms of liturgical music still takes place, albeit informally. In this way, we can maintain that the ultimate author of worship-music is the Church. And who is the Church's "audience"? With whom does the composer share? To whom does the composer communicate experience? To the entire worshipping community, the Church *in toto*.

Pursuant to the above point, I propose that the Church's music is not only an artistic expression of worship but also a function of the Church's teaching role, in that worship-music teaches something of the faith to those who perform or hear it. If the music is prayer indeed, one who worships through music not only "talks to God" but listens and replies to the deity.[9] This point may be clarified by way of example: when an individual Christian who may not necessarily conceive

8. Karl Gustav Fellerer, **The History of Catholic Church Music** (Baltimore: Helicon Press, 1961), p. 197. Also cf. William J. Leonard, ed., **The New Instruction for American Pastors on Sacred Music and the Sacred Liturgy** (Boston: McLaughlin and Reilly, 1959).
9. Cf. Guardini, art. cit.

of himself as afflicted by suffering at a particular time prays one of the penitential psalms in the liturgy, two things happen: of course, he as a member of the Church offers his prayer for those members who are especially afflicted by suffering at that time; at the same time, he himself is able to know more profoundly, through the praying of the psalm, something of the nature of the suffering that affects all Christians.

This obviously applies in prayer expressed musically. To cite another example: in singing a beautiful *Alleluia* at Easter, we praise God (literally, as *Alleluia* is derived from the Hebrew *hallel Yahweh*).[10] Simultaneously, we learn in that experience the joy that prevails in the entire Christian community in light of Jesus' saving resurrection.

Now, which comes first, words or music? This obviously resembles the old riddle about the chicken and the egg. However, in Church music generally we can safely posit the pre-eminence of the word both as theological principle and as applied to the development of worship-music, wherein chants and other melodies become vehicles for the expression of verbal prayers usually developed from Scripture or codified liturgical texts. In this regard, the liturgical musician's endeavor in text selection has tended to be essentially non-melodic, although the composer will obviously consider the suitability of text to melody and may even make minor adjustments therein.[11] While the cultural developments of the ages have allowed great variety of expression in liturgical music, we are frequently reminded that liturgical music must

---

10. Cf. John L. McKenzie, **Dictionary of the Bible** (Milwaukee: Bruce Publishing Company, 1965), p. 21.
11. We are not considering here the many pieces of instrumental music which, although they may foster worshipful expression, are not as such properly liturgical in the strict sense, i.e., they do not convey the texts of the liturgy.

always be a vehicle, never an obstacle, to the expression of prayer. The point is made quite graphically in the tract *De incertitudine et vanitate scientiarum et artium* published at Cologne in 1532:

> Today music has such great license in churches that even along with the canon of the Mass certain obscene little ditties sometimes have equal share; and even the divine offices themselves and the sacred prayers and petitions are performed by lascivious musicians hired at great price, not to make the hearers understand or for the elevation of the spirit, but to incite wanton prurience, not with human voices but with the cries of beasts: boys whining the descant, some bellow the tenor, others bark the counterpoint, others gnash the alto, others moo the bass: the result is that a multitude of sounds is heard, but of the words and prayers not a syllable is understood; the authority of judgment is withdrawn from ears and mind alike.[12]

This forceful statement of *lamentabili* clearly has in mind the sort of norms for liturgical music which appear to have pervailed in a more pristine era in Christian history, and to be restored somewhat during the Gregorian revival begun in the twentieth century under Pope St. Pius X. While it would be myopic to claim that only Gregorian chant could fulfill the needs of worship-music, one is inclined to have special appreciation for its value when considering these principles stated by St. Bernard of Clairvaux (1090-1153):

> Let the chant be full of gravity; let it be neither worldly nor too rude and poor . . . Let it be sweet, yet without levity, and, while it pleases the ear, let it move the heart. It should alleviate sadness, and calm the angry spirit. It should not contradict the sense of the words, but rather enhance it. For it is no slight loss of spiritual grace to be distracted from the profit of the sense by the beauty of the chant, and to have our attention drawn on a mere vocal display, when we ought to be thinking of what is sung.[13]

12. Quoted in Alec Robertson, "Christian Music", **The Twentieth Century Encyclopedia of Catholicism,** 125 (New York: Hawthorn Books, 1961), p. 95.
13. Ibid., p. 42.

An Agonizing Reappraisal

When the modern Gregorian revival received the support of Pope Pius XII's encyclical letter *Musicae sacrae disciplina*,[14] this type of argument was both very much in mind and very much enhanced. As had been observed many a time, worship-music had to be sacramental in the best sense of the word, calling attention not to itself, but to a deeper reality, the relationship in which God calls man to himself in Salvation-History.

The point of the Gregorian revival was never to condemn the great composers of the ages in the history of Catholic worship. A number of those had elaborated on Gregorian or other plainchant motifs, and some of them had worked with idioms quite different. The main point, though, was whether or not their musical expressions in fact illustrated or obfuscated the centrality of the saving mysteries of the liturgy, or whether or not the music served as the music of worship or the music of concert. H. A. Reinhold exemplifies this delicate tension in his famous book *The Dynamics of Liturgy:*

> Just a little more than thirty-two years ago I spent a weekend in Salzburg, Austria. After saying my private Mass in St. Peter's Abbey Church . . . I walked over to the cathedral . . . to assist at a Pontifical Mass where one of the great Mozart Masses with solos and orchestra was to be sung. People of all faiths, in their tourist best, crowded the pews for the Kyrie and the magnificent and wonderfully executed Gloria, deeply enraptured by the musical treat and, I am sure, in a religious and sacred mood. Many of them went out for coffee and a smoke, and then came quietly back to listen to the Credo, the Sanctus, the Agnus Dei and a motet by the great master. Many music lovers who were also worshipers stayed with the celebrating bishop, who looked rather deserted and neglected in the far-away sanctuary of the largest church north of the Alps. That was music in Church.
>
> I have seen tourists in St. Peter's at Rome act in the same way during the Lamentations on Holy Thursday, quieting down for a

14. **AAS** XLVIII (1956): 5-25.

Palestrina responsory or a solo by one of the glorious boy sopranos, silent and standing still in awe. Then the moment the singing flattens out into the rapid recitation of the psalms, the murmur of conversation and the movement of groups starts again. Music in Church.

But then think of Solesmes . . . our American Abbeys . . . with their fine Gregorian plain chant; the perfection of their music is nearly flawless and the chaste and sober notes almost force the visiting tourist on his knees; and he would feel that the attitude of the tourists at Salzburg was impious and worldly.[15]

The principles operative in the renewal of liturgical music earlier in the twentieth century necessarily led to a host of ambiguous situations of delicate balance. One could, after all, become an impious tourist in the pursuit of a well-chanted Gregorian Mass. But the point Reinhold made implies that while such a thing is indeed possible, the nature of the music makes it less likely than in the instance of such a grandiose composition as Beethoven's *Missa Solemnis*. Thus the Gregorian revival would not be limited to plainchant alone; it would encourage as well a variety of traditional and modern compositions of considerable musical complexity and grandeur which could enhance worship, and disapprove of others which would "get in the way" of liturgical worship. Often these latter were not discouraged outright, but channelled in the direction more appropriate to them, the sacred concert as specifically different in nature and purpose from the liturgical service. The Gregorian revival, indeed, would admit to the liturgical worship of the Church such composers as Jean Langlais, Flor Peeters and Joseph Gelineau, to name only a few, but only insofar as those drew attention to and not away from the liturgy which centers on the sacrificial banquet table of Jesus.

The Gregorian revival can be said to have reached its

15. H. A. Reinhold, **The Dynamics of Liturgy** (New York: Macmillan, © 1961), p. 94.

peak around 1960, i.e., mid-way between *Musicae sacrae disciplina* and the advent of sung Mass in the vernacular. Shortly after the new decade of the 1960s began, those who had earnestly tried to lead the movement began to know the futility of teaching grass-roots congregations to chant *Credo III* at Sunday high Mass. At the same time, many were working with or learning of vernacular settings of the liturgical texts (e.g., those of Dennis Fitzpatrick) which, even if they were not to be used right away, seemed harbingers of a vernacular sung Mass around the corner; this sort of thing would give pause to anyone about to launch a congregational *Missa cantata* in the early 1960s. For many there was no tangible evidence that the Gregorian revival would either fail or be superseded, but there did abound rumors of change, which characteristically elicited the response of "Let's not do anything until we hear from Rome!" (Just as well, probably, in many cases where a Latin sung Mass program would likely have died a-borning.)

The 1958 *Instruction* issued by the Sacred Congregation of Rites under Pope Pius XII to deal with questions concerning congregational participation in spoken and sung worship[16] envisioned the congregational *Missa cantata* (down to antiphonal chanting of the Mass Propers) as ideal, but saw this as the culmination of preparatory stages (singing of the simple responses, then the shorter parts of the Ordinary, e.g., *Kyrie, Sanctus, Agnus Dei,* then the *Gloria* and *Credo*). In a "low" Mass *(Missa lecta)* the *Instruction* envisioned spoken participation by the congregation in the same parts of the Mass, according to a similarly calibrated scale of less difficult and more difficult degrees of participation. Even the spoken involvement of the congregation in *Missa lecta* (or *Missa recitata*) was too difficult for

16. Cf. Leonard, ed., op. cit.

most parochial situations, and was opted with consistency only in a number of Catholic schools and other special congregations. Any degree of participation of a more spectacular nature was just that: spectacular, so much so that pilgrims would come from hundreds of miles away to witness and participate in the liturgy at such "shrines" as Monsignor Hillenbrand's Sacred Heart Parish in Hubbard Woods (Winnetka), Illinois.[17]

But there emerged a *tertium quid* (if that Latinism may be allowed) for the use of "popular religious song" during "low Mass" to assist the devotion of the faithful, all the while taking care to stipulate that this was not liturgical music in the proper sense (since it was not in Latin and/or utilized words other than the actual texts of the liturgy). In many a congregation (if the 1958 *Instruction* was even known of) this meant mere ratification of the customary practice of the choir singing "O Lord I Am Not Worthy" at Communion or a motet during the Offertory in "low Mass". But in more imaginative quarters, the way was paved for what the Germans call *Betsingmesse* (or "pray-and-sing Mass"),[18] in which the congregation participates in the Mass in vernacular spoken and sung prayer (technically, of course, participating *alongside* the Mass).

Betsingmesse in its conventional form involved congregational singing at the Entrance, Offertory, Communion and Dismissal times of the Mass. For this purpose the more commonly used hymnals were new ones like *Our Parish*

17. As a case in point, my own experience as a visitor there during Holy Week in 1963: while it was my fortune to be a house guest of a friend in the parish, I learned that people coming from miles around had literally jammed hotels, motels and trailer-park areas in the locality on the north shore of Lake Michigan above Chicago.

18. By the time of the 1958 **Instruction** (specifically released to American Bishops and pastors) the **Betsingmesse** apparently enjoyed the status of "immemorial custom" among Germans. Cf. **Transformation in Christ**, pp. 22, 40.

Prays and Sings or *Peoples Mass Book* that presented "new" hymns—actually venerable in Christian tradition—which were more theologically sound and musically attractive than the "tear-jerkers" of the nineteenth century. And even some of the more "traditional" hymnals underwent some revision during these times, as did the *St. Basil's Hymnal*, wherein the editors explained in their 1958 revised edition:

> Many who have used the **St. Basil's Hymnal** in the past will look in vain for some of the "good, old hymns." These have been passed over by the (editorial) committee because, as has been observed, they are really neither **good** nor **old**. The majority of them reflect the sentimental, individualistic piety of the late Victorian period. Too frequently, their melodies are poor copies of the secular music of that era, while their texts unduly emphasize the human nature of the Savior, tending to bring God to a purely human level rather than to lift man's thoughts to God. Such hymns are more than dated; they are positively harmful in that they attempt to express a religious emotion which is exaggerated, over-familiar and, eventually, false, since they teach the singer to pray badly. In the present collection, then, they have yielded place to **better**, and in some cases **older** hymns of genuine dignity.[19]

So it was that there began to take place in our liturgy such hymns as "Praise to the Lord" and "At the Lamb's High Feast" at the Entrance; "Lord Accept the Gifts We Offer"[20] and "Accept, Almighty Father" at the Offertory; "Humbly We Adore Thee *(Adoro Te Devote)*" and "Where Charity and Love Prevail" or "At That First Eucharist" for Communion; and "Now Thank We All Our God" or Old Hundredth ("Praise God From Whom All Blessings Flow"/"From All That Dwell Below the Skies") as a Recessional.[21]

Furthermore, there was renewed emphasis on the psalms as liturgical prayer, not only in the Mass "Propers" of the

19. **St. Basil's Hymnal** (Cincinnati, Ohio: Ralph Jusko Publications, Inc., 1959), p. v.
20. Commonly sung to the **Tantum Ergo** melody.
21. These are perhaps the most common examples of vernacular hymns that

"high Mass", but in the vernacular renditions of composers like Joseph Gelineau[22] and Stephen Somerville,[23] and later Dennis Fitzpatrick.[24] Advocates of the "Gelineau Psalms" were usually quick to insist that they were not intended as replacements for the Church's *official* liturgical music, which was obviously Gregorian chant in Latin.[25] Indeed, Gelineau and Somerville psalms were generally not used in place of the "Propers", since there would be no point or opportunity in this regard at "low Mass". Rather, they tended to be used (often in some combination with the sort of popular hymns mentioned above) for Entrance, Offertory, Communion or Recessional songs at *Betsingmesse*, as well as for a variety of occasional uses beyond those parameters.

But some composers went further. A prime example is Dennis Fitzpatrick, who developed his vernacular psalm-and-refrain settings for antiphonal singing with a congregation while working his way through DePaul University's

became popular for "low Mass" during the late 1950s and early 1960s, in addition to the old "Holy God, We Praise Thy Name" which was commonly used as a recessional for Benediction and sometimes for Mass as well.

22. Joseph Gelineau, **Twenty-four Psalms and a Canticle** (Toledo, Ohio: Gregorian Institute of America, 1955), tr. and comp. by Gregory Murray and Clifford Howell. This is an American edition of the English translation from the French first released in England by the Ladies of the Grail; it was followed by an edition of **Thirty Psalms and Two Canticles** by Pere Gelineau shortly thereafter.
23. Somerville's psalms were published in this country by World Library of Sacred Music, Cincinnati, Ohio, in various editions.
24. Cf. Dennis Fitzpatrick, ed., **Demonstration English Liturgy Altar Missal** (Evanston, Illinois: Friends of the English Liturgy, 1963) and **English Liturgy Hymnal** (Chicago, Illinois: F.E.L. Publishing Company, 1965). During the second session of Vatican Council II, the English-speaking Bishops at the Council received copies of Fitzpatrick's Altar Missal and LP records of his **Demonstration English Mass** (in which I took part) as examples of how a Missa cantata could be rendered in English. Those Bishops who reacted at all (about 10%) were quite favorably impressed.
25. Cf. Wills, **Bare Ruined Choirs**, p. 58.

school of music as a parish organist-choirmaster in Chicago in the early 1960s. Taking note of the receptivity to his music evinced by the parochial schoolchildren at their daily Mass, Fitzpatrick used his psalms and refrains with them at the Entrance, Offertory and Communion times of the Mass, in which instances it was surely no chore to incorporate the psalm-verses pertinent to the Proper of the liturgical feast being celebrated. In yet a further stage of development, Fitzpatrick devised for "low Mass" use vernacular chants for the *Kyrie, Gloria, Credo, Sanctus* and *Agnus Dei* in which he would lead the congregation while the celebrant (usually pacing himself with some care) officiated over the liturgy in Latin. (This practice, imitated by Fitzpatrick's colleagues in some Chicago and Milwaukee parishes, came to be called a *Fitzmesse* or "the Fitzpatrician Rite").[26] Some hailed this sort of technique for its involvement of the congregation (especially children) in a sung liturgy utilizing the vernacular. Others damned it as a shameless circumvention of liturgical norms, and a virtual replacement of the celebrating priest by the singing-director or cantor as leader of the People of God at worship.

To advocates and critics alike, various forms of *Betsingmesse* could be no more than a stopgap. Even some who hoped for eventual vernacularization of the liturgy felt they could not countenance such widespread use of vernacular popular song when the liturgy, officially, remained in Latin.[27]

26. Some others who utilized Fitzpatrick's antiphonal psalms-and-refrains and even parts of his English Mass ordinary were Thomas McGuire at St. John the Evangelist Parish in San Francisco, Roger Nachtwey and Richard Weber at the Church of the Gesu and St. Rose of Lima Parish, both in Milwaukee, Edward Dixon in various Chicago parishes, David Njaa at Sacred Heart Parish ("Hilly's") in Winnetka, Illinois, and Donald Wimmer and myself at the Gesu and St. Rose of Lima in Milwaukee, then later at Seton Hall University.
27. One such person at the time (1963) was Rev. Richard Sherburne, S.J., then moderator of a student liturgical group at Marquette University

And some who loved the American *Betsingmesse* could not be wholly satisfied by a ritual that tended to isolate celebrant from congregation rather than unite the two. Something had to come to solve the problem. One alternative which seemed to have been considered seriously in some quarters was a prohibition of such wide use of vernacular song as was taking place in the *Fitzmesse* and other situations.[28] The other alternative, of course, could come only from Rome: official vernacularization of the liturgy, at least in part. The latter, of course, is just what took place in the wake of the Second Vatican Council's second session, whence emanated the Dogmatic Constitution *Sacrosanctum Concilium* (On the Sacred Liturgy), promulgated on December 4, 1963, for implementation the following November in the United States.[29]

Of course, implementation would be piecemeal. At first, vernacular would be utilized only for some parts of the Mass "pertaining to the people". The result would be a

known as **Manus Dei.** Father Sherburne (himself a Latin professor) insisted that the University Mass in the Church of the Gesu and other functions of **Manus Dei** should foster congregational participation in the liturgy in Latin only, since that was the official liturgy of the Church then obtaining. Thus that mode of participation prevailed at liturgies under the aegis of **Manus Dei** at the Gesu, and the "Fitzpatrician Rite" at those liturgies where the task was entrusted to Nachtwey, Weber and myself.

28. Archbishop William Cousins of Milwaukee forbade "low" services during Holy Week, 1964. It might have been argued that this was done so as to guarantee that adequate emphasis and solemnity be given to the celebration of the liturgy during Holy Week, but I suspect it was really to prevent use of the vernacular "Fitzpatrician Rite" at St. Rose of Lima Parish.
29. Walter M. Abbott, ed., **The Documents of Vatican II** (New York: American Press, Association Press and Guild Press, 1966), pp. 137ff.

liturgy which oscillated between the liturgical language of old and the new vernacular in a fashion which was hardly satisfactory to anyone, and confusing to almost everyone. It would be some time yet before the vernacular would be used for all the parts of the liturgy said by the congregations or heard by them.[30] In the mean time, it was understood that sung Mass would continue in Latin while the use of vernacular hymns would be explicitly encouraged for "low Mass". For all practical purposes, this meant about a year and a half of liturgical limbo: composers were unable to use new English Mass arrangements for the liturgy; publishers were not altogether sure if the texts would change again for sung Mass in the vernacular; some musicians and others dedicated to the Latin *Missa cantata* continued to urge the singing of the "high Mass" in Latin, and even the learning and performance of new Latin sung Masses, before the inevitable transition to a liturgy both spoken and sung in the vernacular.[31]

Alongside the advent of vernacularization in liturgical language came a movement for the modernization or diversification of liturgical music forms. Prior to the era of Vatican Council II, there had been some careful attempts at expressing reverent worship in modern forms that were judged by their adherence to—or at least lack of affront to —traditional standards (Russell Woollen's *Mass in the Major*

---

30. Cf. Chapter 3, supra.
31. In the Archdiocese of Newark, the chancery office was rumored to be so strict about not allowing sung Mass in English before Easter Sunday of 1966 that an English sung Mass that I had prepared for a convocation on Wednesday of Holy Week at Seton Hall University (not knowing the policy of the chancery office to be such) was cancelled by the University. When I asked if the Archbishop could be approached to see if he might interpret the situation favorably (it was, after all, the student body "Easter convocation Mass" before going on vacation), I was told that the chance of this being effective was virtually nil, so it should not even be tried.

5

Modes is an example, as would be Jean Langlais' organ solo *Incantation for a Holy Day*). But in the early 1960s, new musical expressions began to enter the picture. One of these, "borrowed" from the Anglicans, was the "Twentieth Century Folk Mass" by Beaumont; sometimes mislabeled as a "jazz Mass", this attempt was really something out of the 1940s movie musicals, and generally dismissed as narrow in scope and superficial. Another, by Anglican priest Ian Mitchell, worked more in the "folk" idiom of guitar music becoming popular on American campuses during the early sixties. Yet another, developed under Roman Catholic missionaries in Africa, was the *Missa Luba,* utilizing native chants and instruments (including African drums) for the Latin *Missa cantata*. None of these managed to make a lasting impact on the Catholic liturgy. Beaumont's work had misfired, and *Missa Luba* was becoming obsolete almost upon its release to the western world. But while Mitchell's work did not manage to command lasting attention, it did serve as a forerunner of what was to come in Roman Catholic liturgical "folk" music.

The venture which is considered to have pioneered "folk" music for American Catholic liturgical worship is *The American Mass Program,* composed by a black priest in Cincinnati named Clarence Joseph Rivers and published by World Library of Sacred Music in the same city in 1964.[32] Rivers' work is believed to have borrowed heavily from other music, (e.g., his prayer-of-the-faithful litany lifts directly from Gelineau's Ps 135, and his "God Is Love" is often compared melodically to "Blow, Gabriel, Blow".) Not long after "The Rivers Mass" (not actually a Mass but a series of liturgical songs) made its impact on the American Church, Dennis

---

32. Cf. my reference to the introduction of this program at Grailville in 1963, in Chapter 4, supra.

Fitzpatrick as publisher brought out the folk songs of Ray Repp and Sister Germaine under the aegis of his F.E.L. Church Publications.[33] For Fitzpatrick, as for many new liturgical composers, this signalled an ironic turn of events. Some of the work they had done that would be considered more "serious" or "substantial" would be ignored by the liturgical *aggiornamento,* like Fitzpatrick's *Demonstration English Mass.* Those who would survive in the field at all, like Fitzpatrick, would do so by adapting quickly to the vicissitudes of a wholly new "market" for liturgical music that would demand "folk Mass" material almost as rapidly as it could be produced.

What happened, between 1963 and 1967, was that the Church leapfrogged from a musical diet of *Missa cantata* with occasional English hymns for "low Mass" to an infatuation with "folk" Mass hymns, without stopping in between to consider the sung Mass in the vernacular at all seriously or thoroughly. This meant that Fitzpatrick and others (like Harry Gunther, for example) who had prepared for the rendering of "high Mass" in English would find that they had been working on a product unwanted by most of the American Church. Under such circumstances, there would still be much use of the "low Mass" hymns borrowed from the hymnals of our Protestant brothers, and even for some of the older pieces of music in the Catholic repertoire for choral or congregational use. But *Missa cantata,* once vernacularized, seemed suddenly to die. Once removed from Rome in language, the American Church removed itself from Rome in ritual atmosphere as well, and the austere, the splendid, the solemn, the carefully executed all seemed to give way to the

---

33. The name comes from Friends of the English Liturgy, the original designation for the publishing firm since it was founded on donations from a number of "friends" sympathetic to Fitzpatrick's endeavors in English liturgical music. Cf. **Transformation in Christ,** p. 17, fn. 3.

"pop", the streamlined, the "instant", the "funky".

My intent here is not to demean the folk-Mass literature of the mid-1960s. Some of it was quite good, but most of it could not be: it was produced too quickly, under too much pressure, by too many people, in far too short a time to bring about a very high "batting average" musically. A lot of it, to be sure, was determined to express emotion in the most "relevant" (read *instantaneous* or *uninhibited*) terms possible. This sort of thing, if manifestly an excess, was eminently understandable. It was, in a way, a natural reaction to the enforced subtlety and detachment of Roman Catholic liturgical music before the era of Vatican II. Ironically, the very Gregorian revival that threatened the nineteenth-century "tear-jerkers" of the Latin liturgy was about to give way, by way of pendular movement, to the new "tear-jerkers" of the folk-Mass idiom.[34]

This meant that folk-hymns like "Take Our Bread (We Love You)", "My Lord Will Come Again (. . ."He'll take my hand and we'll go home . . ."), "We Are Your Bread Now" (to the tune of "Waltzing Matilda") and "We Are All Joined in Christ" (to "Edelweiss") would become the coin of the realm in the renewal of liturgical music in the late 1960s. This does not mean that such music was typical of liturgical celebrations at this time. For many liturgies, there would be no music at all (as before the Council), or a "low Mass" with four "conventional" hymns (e.g., "Praise to the Lord", etc.). But that, of course, was hardly new. In terms of what *was* new, the "folk-Mass" carried the day. And its impact was by no means limited to liturgies for youngsters. Many a parish found that older parishioners preferred

---

34. For a more detailed exposition of my views on this matter, cf. my monthly columns on liturgical music which ran in **The Advocate** (Newark, N.J.), in their "Topic" magazine section, from 1967 through 1970.

the "folk Mass" to traditional worship patterns, and not a few organists found themselves belting out a "folk" hymn (written for guitar, of course) on the parish calliope.

Of course, not even the "folk Mass" music was really new, in most cases. Even if it was not directly borrowed part for part (as with Sebastian Temple's "The Mass Is Ended", curiously identical to a Regal Pale Beer jingle that made the rounds of Northern California in the late 1940s), it was essentially a repetition of what had happened in the latter part of the nineteenth century (as lamented by the editors of the new *Saint Basil's Hymnal*, supra):[35] melodic patterns tended to be adapted from the less complex and difficult secular music of the time to express a series of sentimental fantasies concerning the relationship between the worshipper as individual suffering in this vale of tears and a Jesus whose human nature was extrapolated out of all proportion to his divine nature.

In a curious fashion, the "liberalization" of liturgical form worked very much against the liturgical "liberals" who longed for it. As Garry Wills has perceptively noted in his book *Bare Ruined Choirs*, the liturgical liberalism of the decade just before Vatican Council II was not directed against the Roman liturgical tradition *in toto*, but against those abuses of it which degraded the liturgy with their maudlin and inept expressions. "The Catholic liberal would be more in love with incense than any altar boy; yet he would intellectualize his incense in a congenial setting . . . It was not Rome he disliked in his churches, it was Peoria."[36] In most "folk" liturgies, there would be Peoria aplenty.

35. Cf. fn. 19, supra.; loc. cit.
36. Wills, op. cit., p. 39.

At this writing, we seem cut adrift from Rome and Peoria alike, in a way. While we have surely not preserved the pre-Conciliar forms of musical worship on any grand scale, we are not so boxed into the folk-Mass rage as we were in the late 1960s. Most of the good features of the folk-Mass experience, thank God, seem to be surviving. Most of the aspects of it that were merely superficial and transitory, or just downright awful, are on the wane (equal gratitude to the deity for this). As recently as five years ago, were a group of my college students to experience (i.e., hear and/or sing) a Joe Wise or Sebastian Temple folk-hymn, most of them would be enchanted by it and a few would even have tears of emotion running down their cheeks; today, most of them yawn and a few even wince. We are making progress.

But if we are seeing the end of an era when the git-fiddle ditties of today have occupied the place of the ballroom heart-throbs of yesteryear in the cultivation of popular liturgical music, it will hardly be enough to take comfort in what *bad* music is *not* holding sway. We must, rather, ask ourselves what music can be utilized today and for some time to come so that through it the People of God may worship.

In this regard it will be necessary to remember that circumstances and needs will doubtless vary from time to time and from place to place, and that myriad problems will call for a host of different solutions. But it must also be noted that there are some principles that must apply generally if the People of God are truly to worship through music: 1) We must more carefully guarantee the relationship between sung prayer and the texts of the sacred liturgy; 2) we must more judiciously seek a balance between music that is contemporary and traditional, "easy" and "difficult", simple and complex, etc.; 3) we must more prudently oversee the balance between musical prayer the congregation takes direct part in and worship-music the congregation *hears*.

1. *The relationship between sung prayer and liturgical texts.*

Time was, not too long ago, when nothing could be sung to suffice for the *Introit, Gradual, Alleluia, Offertory* or *Communion* of a Mass that was not identical textually, both in language (Latin) and in verbal content, without stepping outside the boundaries of what constituted properly a *Missa cantata*. Then the language requirement was relaxed in the wake of *Sacrosanctum Concilium* and subsequent instructions, and it became possible to render a kosher vernacular version of the "Proper" (but again, verbatim, according to approved translations).[37] Now, since the *Ordo Missae* promulgated by Pope Paul VI in 1970, it is permissible, even somewhat encouraged, to perform a musical selection in place of any of the "proper" parts of the Mass even if it does not coincide even closely in text, so long as it generally corresponds to either the theme of the liturgical "proper" in question or the particular part of the Mass involved (e.g., Entrance, Offertory, Communion).[38] This leaves pastors and musicians a lot of latitude. Perhaps too much. Ironically enough, in an age when we have just reworked our temporal and sanctoral liturgical cycles, and reexamined the appropriateness of our series of Scriptural texts for the liturgical feasts of the year, we are now allowing such leeway with the "propers" that the theme of a particular celebration

37. The Liturgical Commissions of the Archdiocese of New York, The Diocese of Brooklyn and the Diocese of Rockville Centre, comp., **A Handbook for the Revised Roman Liturgy** (New York: 1970), hereinafter cited as **Handbook**, p. 35.
38. Ibid., pp. 34-38.

need not really be implied in the sung prayer of the liturgy. According to the *Ordo Missae,* it is literally possible for a congregation to ignore the specific proper parts of the Mass on Sunday after Sunday (and, if they are so inclined, even weekday after weekday) by singing again and again the same hymns, e.g., "Praise to the Lord" at the Entrance procession; "Lord, Accept the Gifts We Offer" or "Take Our Bread" at the Offertory; "Whatsoever You Do" at Communion. One could go even further and supply a stock *Alleluia* after the first reading, possibly (although not necessarily) joined with another stock element or two to make the transition between Scriptural readings.

Now, what is really so wrong with that, anyway? For once or so every month, probably not much. But if this type of thing—or anything like it—takes place day in and day out or week in and week out for sheer lack of imagination or industry, then we seriously sabotage the teaching mission of the liturgy and of the proper liturgical texts; we also seriously sabotage the magisterial function of worship-music as it has been described earlier in this chapter.

This does not mean for a moment that I prefer the sing-song "recitation" of the Mass propers to a viable musical alternative. I am merely suggesting that most of the musical alternatives we might be tempted to use today are more convenient than viable, in that pastors (more often, those whom pastors deputize to oversee liturgical music) do not take sufficient care to see that anything chosen for worship-music correspond as much and as explicitly as possible to the liturgy of the day, rather than be just "a general Entrance hymn", or whatever. The "general" hymn expressing the meaning of the Entrance, Offertory or Communion will surface often enough, simply owing to lack of time or preparation or expertise, but if we allow ourselves to consider it normative, our chances of achieving more than that to any significant degree become slight indeed.

I am suggesting, then, that we take particular heed of the notion of the Psalter as prayerbook of the Church (Yes, Garry Wills—spoken like a true "fifties liberal Catholic"!) I suggest further that there is a grace of the Spirit somehow present in the plan and placement of the liturgical "propers". This does not mean that the Spirit ossifies liturgical texts, so that they may never be changed or deviated from. It does mean, though, that the Spirit is present not only in the revising and reconsidering of liturgical texts, but in their present dispensation at this stage of development, and we would be ill-advised to simply ignore that, not only for its own merit, but also for its potential as a visible union with our fellow members of the *communio sanctorum* (something we seem to be missing a bit of today, I fear). This will often mean looking to the psalmody of composers like Gelineau, Somerville, Deiss, Fitzpatrick and Gunther (the latter having worked out his system in light of the new *Graduale Simplex*) for the selection of worship-music at the appropriate intervals in the liturgy, rather than simply falling back upon a category of "Advent hymns" or "Communion hymns", or whatever. This does not mean that we will not have cause to opt — say —"O Come, O Come, Emmanuel" during Advent, or "At That First Eucharist" during Communion. It only means that we will do so after having searched out alternatives, much as my wife falls back upon a dinner of hamburger only after other possibilities have been considered and found impracticable.

If we strive for this, we will not always achieve total success, but I believe we will have managed to bring to our liturgical celebrations a new sort of atmosphere which will be more mindful of the Service of the Word and therefore of the Word made Flesh in each liturgy. It also means we will find ourselves more mindful of the moods expressed to and through the worshipping community in different liturgical celebrations. One of my complaints about the excesses of the late-1960s "folk Mass" binge (over which I officiated in large measure as a collegiate liturgist) is that it tended to obfuscate the distinctions between very definite liturgical seasons. While it seems true that the elimination of the *Alleluia* during Lent and the *Gloria Patri* during Passiontide might have been a bit artificial in an age where we know that the Lord is truly risen, there was a point to it all: to make our liturgical year a series of *arses* and *theses* (if I may use that Gregorian term here!) highlighting different moods or facets of Christian life in light of Jesus' saving passion, death *and* resurrection, and their implications for the followers of Jesus. However, much of the liturgical spirit in the latter part of the 1960s moved in the direction of singing the "happy-happy" songs every week and day of the liturgical year—replete with multiple *Alleluias* (or perhaps more likely *Allelus!*) in such wise that the motifs of liturgical seasons were virtually lost. It is true that we are not members of a monastic or medieval society where all of human life is presumed to be conducted in accord with the liturgical calendar of the Roman Church. Yet that calendar is not altogether without meaning or purpose and we frustrate whatever meaning or purpose might reside therein by any cavalier ignorance of liturgical feasts and seasons as having definite and different meanings and moods to be expressed through worship-music.

2. *Balance between styles of music.*

It will follow logically from the above that we cannot achieve our goals with only one type of liturgical music expression. Most of our more Scripturally-oriented selections would be a bit too difficult as a steady repertoire for many a parish choir, let alone a congregation. Besides, even a good command of Gelineau or Fitzpatrick or Gunther by a particular worshipping community would lead to monotony. On the other hand, much of our "folk-Mass" music, beautiful for its freshness and simplicity in many cases, is hindered to a large extent by its very lack of complexity and profundity. Finally, if worship-music exercises to some degree a *teaching* function in the Church as total believing and worshipping community, then do we not frustrate the very purpose of educating and building up the People of God[39] if we are satisfied to bring them only one style of worship-music?

It will become clear that we will not get off so easily as to have "traditional" hymns for the "old folks" and "guitar" hymns for the "youngsters", and so on. Such approaches not only fail to really deal with the problems mentioned above, but also do not achieve the educative function of liturgical music, in that they allow a group to stagnate into only one mode of expression, promoting ignorance or even intolerance of other modes of expression (the young people's group that hears nothing but folk music can be just as badly off as the group that never hears it).

It will be clear, too, that the ends we are seeking, viz., expression of liturgical feasts and seasons, highlighting of different parts of the Mass (Offertory, Communion, etc.) and the active and intelligent participation—interior and exterior—of the faithful, cannot be subsumed under the heading of one style of liturgical music *per omnia saecula saeculorum,* or even for the proverbial month of Sundays.

Sometimes, for one or another of the good reasons above, we may opt for the antiphonal psalm-and-refrain, another time, with equally reasonable conviction, the "traditional"

---

39. Cf. Ep 4:1-5:20; I am of course juxtaposing the Pauline image pertaining to the **Body of Christ** with Vatican II's **People of God.**

hymn or the "folk" song. And some of these may be musically familiar and simple, while others—appropriate as they may be for liturgical use—may be quite difficult indeed, almost in proportion to their very beauty and fittingness. Which brings us, of course, to the next point: we must strive to effect:

3. *Balance between the congregation singing and hearing.*

In a symposium sponsored by the Liturgical Conference some years ago, the famous Monsignor Schmitt who led the choir at Boys' Town asked, rhetorically, if liturgical participation by the congregation meant that everyone had to sing everything all the time. He then went on to answer his own academic question in the negative.[40] Both within the framework of that particular symposium, and in the Church generally, there have been those who would be wont to reply to Schmitt by insisting that the congregation should sing as much as possible in the worship-music of the Church, so as to ensure that full and active participation of theirs which *Sacrosanctum Concilium* insists be valued above all else.[41] I sympathize with this latter group, not only for their faithfulness to a Conciliar constitution, but also because they serve as a check on those who might presume (as they felt Monsignor Schmitt might) that the congregation really isn't capable of participating very much in a sung liturgy. However, the Monsignor had a point: it is not necessary for everyone to sing everything all the time in order to have substantial participation by the congregation in sung worship. Furthermore, I submit, we have perhaps frustrated the very

40. The Liturgical Conference, comp., **Crisis in Church Music?** (Washington, D.C.: The Liturgical Conference, 1967).
41. Cf. Abbott, op. cit., **Sacrosanctum Concilium**, #14. Obviously, this injunction admits of exaggeration or misinterpretation.

ends of such participation by trying to make too many people sing too many parts of the sung liturgy too many times in too many situations.

Make no mistake! For almost a decade and a half I have been an ardent supporter or an active leader of congregational participation in sung worship. It is precisely *for* that reason that I believe such participation will best be enhanced when there prevails a proper complementarity between worship-music that the congregation sings and worship-music that the congregation hears. There is surely need for both in our liturgy.

To draw an analogy: a book will be hard to follow if all of its contents are in plain type, with no boldface and no italics, no headings, and so on. But a book is just as lacklustre if all its contents are in italic type, or boldface, or whatever. There must be contrast for the sake of subtle emphasis. This means that a congregation ought to *hear* some things, *say* some things, and *sing* some things. Furthermore, we should realize that our congregation will not be drawn to worship through music if they are so preoccupied with the technicalities of the music that they cannot utilize it as what it should be, a vehicle toward or expression of a natural outgrowth of an interior attitude or disposition to worship.

If we are at all honest, we should realize that Americans are not a nation of singers. We are inclined to *listen* to the national anthem sung by a professional soloist at the ball game or some other public assembly, and to stand at attention in the most patriotic of moods. But we are not likely to join in the singing. Our patriotism is not diminished by our silence; our silence is simply part of the American tendency to be more spectator than participant in any demonstration of emotion in public. If this is true of an America whose roots in general are largely Anglo-Saxon, then think of

[123]

American *Catholics,* who come from such ethnic backgrounds as the Irish (where, again, it is not fashionable to make displays of emotion in public), the midwest Germans (likewise), the northwestern Scandinavians (similarly), and the Italians, Puerto Ricans, Chicanos and Cubans—among whose cultures it is all right for women to exhibit religious piety, but not the menfolk. The Germans' lot is bettered by their tradition of *Betsingmesse,* of course, and things like the *cursillo* movement have made some impact in the religious lives of Hispanic Catholics. But in large measure, American Catholics are hardly a nation (or an amalgam of nationalities) likely to sing in Church.

This being the case, we should have great sympathy for the congregation (or the leader of congregational singing) who has found the past decade difficult. Beyond a few hymns that *"every*body knows" ("Holy God, We Praise Thy Name", *O Salutaris Hostia, Tantum Ergo,* a few Christmas carols and a smattering of "golden oldies" too maudlin to mention), American Catholics have been finding that they have had to "start from scratch" when it comes to congregational participation in sung worship. Over a period of about ten years (actually, a rather short time, all things considered) we have managed to make about twenty hymns familiar to the average American Catholic congregation (including both "traditional" and "folk" hymns). This is no small achievement, even if it came about from little else than sheer repetition.[42] Had we the foresight to work more

42. The most familiar hymns would vary to some extent from parish to parish, of course, but I would imagine them to be, in most cases, the following (not necessarily in order of popularity or familiarity): "Praise to the Lord"; "Lord, Accept the Gifts We Offer" (to the **Tantum Ergo** melody, thus not altogether new); "Humbly We Adore Thee" (again taken from a chant, in this instance **Adore Te Devote**); "Now Thank We All Our God"; "At That First Eucharist"; "The Church's One Foundation"; "On This Day, the First of Days"; "Sing of Mary, Pure

methodically at it, our congregations' repertoire might be somewhat greater in both quantity and quality, but this is no time to lament lost opportunities. It *is* a time to take stock of where our congregations are at this juncture, and capitalize on this situation for the future enhancement of congregational involvement in worship-music.

Now is the time to realize that we have been indiscriminate in many of our efforts at congregational singing. We have also been fortunate, in many instances, but we cannot repeat our lack of discrimination at a time when American Catholics are wont to exhibit less docility and more critical scrutiny in their liturgical experiences. We are in a position to utilize the general repertoire mentioned above[43] as a sort of "guaranteed minimum" on which to build. In this process, we will doubtless see the retirement of some hymns not meant to endure, eventually to be replaced by others (and some of *those*, in turn, will be of a transitory nature). We will also be in a position to decide just which parts of the liturgy we wish to enjoy the emphasis of full congregational involvement in song, which ones we wish to enjoy the emphasis—no less forceful, but different—of choral rendition, and which ones we wish to enjoy the special emphasis that can be lent by antiphonal singing between

and Lowly"; "Immaculate Mary" (again, not altogether new, but a real improvement over most Marian hymns of yesteryear); "O Come, O Come, Emmanuel" (previously known to many a congregation, but usually just by hearing their parish choirs sing it every Advent); "O Sacred Head" (a similar observation would apply here); "A Mighty Fortress Is Our God"; Old Hundredth ("Praise God From Whom All Blessings Flow"/"From All That Dwell Below the Skies"); "For All the Saints"; "Hear, O Lord", "Shout From the Highest Mountain", "They'll Know We Are Christians By Our Love"; "Whatsoever You Do"; "Keep in Mind . . ." (Deiss); "Sons of God" (Theim); "Take Our Bread . . ."; "We Are All Joined in Christ" (Edelweiss); "What Thou Gavest for the Taking", etc.

---

43. Cf. fn. 42, supra.

congregation and choir or cantor.[44] In this context, we will often find that the hymns known now (plus a few new ones to replace some that are obsolescent) will find themselves in use mostly as recessionals, sometimes as Entrance hymns for particular seasonal feasts (e.g., Marian feasts, etc.) and the like. But we will find entering the picture a greater usage of psalms and refrains (or antiphons) for the "proper" of many a feast, particularly for the Communion and Offertory processions, wherein a cantor or choir can sing the more complex or changeable verses, and the congregation (usually with the help of a congregational-singing leader)[45] can sing a simple antiphon. As a next stage, to lend greater solemnity to the Service of the Word, this technique can be used for the Response after the First Reading and for the Gospel Acclamation. This will necessarily mean the cultivation of choirs not as concert groups, but as special facilitators of congregational involvement in sung worship. Furthermore, it will mean the special cultivation of cantors and directors of congregational singing as liaisons between choir and congregation.

Such an approach should not argue for or lead towards the type of choir-congregation situation that obtained in many a parish prior to the Council's reform of the liturgy. In the wake of Vatican II, certain practices were killed that should indeed have been laid to eternal rest. One of these was the assumption that anything "really important" had to be sung by the choir. Another of these was the notion that

44. I distinguish here between a cantor and a soloist. A cantor enhances the singing of the choir and/or congregation in a representative fashion; a soloist arrogates one or both of these functions to himself in an operatic performance, and thus has a place in something like a concert of sacred music, but not in the liturgy per se.
45. The leader of congregational singing and the cantor can be one and the same person, or two different people, depending on the availability of trained personnel.

the choir comprised a special elite in the congregation (replete with special blazers, as in the case of a parochial "glee club", or special choir robes, as in many Midwestern parishes, etc.). While we do wish to lend proper dignity to choral singing in liturgy, we must be careful that seriousness of purpose and preparation do not degenerate into snobbery and divisiveness, and this will be a difficult situation in which to strike the proper balance. Also, we do not want to lend credence to the assumption that anyone who can sing at all within a congregation "belongs in the choir". The purpose of a choir, as I understand it, is to *facilitate* congregational involvement in sung worship, not *replace* it. Thus a choir should involve only a nucleus, only the number necessary for its function, and should not subsume all those in the parish capable of carrying a tune; the congregation in the pews must include a number of people who can sing, too.[46] Furthermore, we must never think in terms of congregational singing as something "watered-down" from an ideal wherein things to be sung in the liturgy belong properly to the choir alone. More truly, the choir is at most a representative of the congregation, and derives its legitimacy insofar as it really is that, either in antiphonal singing or in the occasional motet or other selection performed by the choir alone.

If we keep in mind some of these principles, we are well on the way to a complementary balance between music heard by and music sung by the congregation, in a truly participated liturgy, in a manner which reflects not only the letter but also the spirit of the liturgical reform begun

---

46. I am not referring here to choir members who act as "plants" or "shills" in the congregation. This technique is usually spotted for what it is by choir-members and congregation alike, and often demoralizes or discourages congregational singing more than encourages it.

under Pope St. Pius X and culminating in the *aggiornamento* of Vatican Council II. Then we will truly be able to say that, with due grounding in Catholic tradition, we are singing a song to the Lord in a fashion that is as fully and legitimately new as this very morning.

CHAPTER SIX

Renewal in the Eucharistic Liturgy

WE HAVE ALREADY considered (in Chapter 4, supra) some principles that are important for liturgical renewal at this stage in our history. Let us now concentrate even more specifically on the implementation of some of these principles with regard to the eucharistic liturgy which is the chief worship-experience for Catholics. It will be clear from the previous treatment that I favor a modicum of flexibility, but within a context of continuity or coherence, for the celebration of the eucharist as the Christian community's proclamation of its identity. Now to elaborate:

In my view the following elements need to be present in any celebration of the eucharist that is to serve as liturgical focus for the Christian community:

1. A Call to Worship, culminating in an Entrance Rite
2. A Penitential Rite
3. A Service of the Word
4. A Eucharistic Sacrifice and Banquet
5. A Thanksgiving-and-dismissal Rite

Surely these can take place within the context of various options, but each of the above should in some way be present in the celebration.

1. *A Call to Worship, culminating in an Entrance Rite.*
The nomenclature will be recognizable to anyone who is familiar with Protestant services in America. My notion here is that of literally calling the community to worship and establishing both the right psychological atmosphere and the

right intellectual predisposition for participation in community worship. While various congregations will strive to achieve this in a variety of ways, it is important that this not be ignored or eliminated. We cannot expect our congregations to enter into a celebration "cold". Even in some of the informal "home" liturgies that have become popular in recent years, it is necessary to effect a transition between the informality that legitimately exists in a home gathering and the special purpose of making eucharist, all the while preserving the intimacy of the community gathered there.

Some congregations, Catholic and Protestant alike, will attempt to create a worshipful atmosphere before the service by means of a carillon or organ prelude, just as some who host "home" liturgies will take care that all present know one another and are comfortable. This is a valuable first step, but it is surely not all. There should also be, as indicated above, the right intellectual predisposition, particularly with regard to the specific celebration about to take place. I envision this taking place as a harbinger of what is to come in the Service of the Word, wherein a leader of the community at worship (the celebrating priest, a deacon, a lay reader) would call the community together to prepare for the celebration that is to begin. Many parishes have been doing this by having a "commentator" or "lector" read a brief explanation of, or exhortation based on, the theme of the day's liturgy. This is a good thing, provided it is done with conviction, with some relation to the community present, and not just "read off" or "recited" in the fashion of "one more announcement".[1] Such a brief period of psycho-

---

1. Many of the Missals published during the late 1950s and early 1960s for congregational use contain this sort of material, as do many of the "commentary" books published thereafter. The same is true of the exegetical notes I have provided for the introduction of each liturgical feast in my series of sermon-outline materials for cycle "A" of the

logical and intellectual preparation before Mass could include the business of instructing the congregation in a new liturgical action to be begun at that celebration, i.e., a new prayer or hymn, *provided that the most careful and judicious sort of economy be brought to bear in this.* This will mean, quite concretely, that the typical congregation will be unable to digest any thematic preparation for a coming celebration of the liturgy if this becomes overwhelmed by a practical drill in the logistics of the liturgy about to begin. Therefore, no more than one new element (be it a new hymn, gesture, spoken prayer or whatever) should be introduced prior to a liturgical celebration, its introduction should be no more than a couple of minutes long ("couple" means two, not five or six), and the introduction of new liturgical elements should not be a weekly experience visited upon the congregation. If these principles are implemented, there will likely be far less frustration, and far more internalization and acceptance, whenever liturgical additions are at issue. Furthermore, whenever such an introduction must take place, it is obviously best if this can somehow be motivated in terms of the specific liturgy about to take place. What follows is an example for a "typical" parish congregation:

(Following whatever musical prelude might have taken place, the leader of community worship[2] addresses his fellow members of the congregation.) "Today we celebrate the liturgy for the First Sunday

liturgical readings, **If I Were to Preach** (Staten Island, N.Y.: Alba House, 1974). However, such materials should never be "swallowed whole" or used indiscriminately and uncritically by local leaders of community worship.

---

2. This would usually be someone whose specific purpose is to lead at least the sung prayer, and maybe also the spoken prayer, of the congregation. In some instances, the same person could be lector or deacon (depending on available personnel). In rare situations (others lacking) this might even be the celebrant.

[131]

of Advent. The imagery of today's Biblical passages, drawn from the Old Testament prophet Isaiah, and from an Epistle of Paul and the Gospel of Matthew in the New Testament, all points in the same direction: the coming of a new kingdom in the Lord Jesus. In the Psalm of the Old Testament chosen by the Church for our sung response, we express this notion in terms of going to the house of the Lord, partaking of the new city he has built. Listen to (the cantor/the choir/me)[3] sing the simple congregational refrain (refrain is sung: "We shall go up with joy to the house of our God"). All right, now let's sing that simple refrain together (the refrain is sung congregationally, and probably repeated once). Fine, so that will be our response to the first reading in today's liturgy. Now let us begin today's celebration with our Entrance Hymn . . ."[4]

In the example just given, a piece of music is introduced to the congregation. It will not always be that way, but this is given as a particular instance of how such an introduction might take place within the context of a *call to worship*. Note that the music being introduced in this example is different from the Entrance Hymn, which is presumably already familiar to the congregation.[5] The introduction of the new piece, or the reinforcement of the familiar Entrance Hymn, can be enhanced by the inclusion of it in the musical prelude (if one is to be played). One thing that is important is that the leader of community worship[6] is functioning liturgically or ministerially, not simply as an announcer of data, an introducer of unwelcome encumbrance, or an unwilling errand-boy for the dictators of liturgical change. However minimally, there is established an atmosphere for the celebration that is to take place, and a disposition toward it.

The call to worship will not always be like this, certainly.

3. Ibid.
4. Cf. the materials offered for the First Sunday of Advent in **If I Were to Preach,** from which this example is taken.
5. Ibid.
6. Cf. fns. 2, 3, supra.

It will vary according to the situation of the congregation, its size, its location and a host of other factors. But the variations on the theme should be easier to envision once a general example is explored, as in the above.

2. A Penitential Rite

The *Ordo Missae* of 1970 provides for three ways in which the Penitential Rite may be conducted.[7] There is little point in elaborating on this here, except to observe the following: when it is decided to utilize that option which includes the litany *Kyrie, eleison . . .*[8] with specific petitions, it is my suggestion that the petitions be as concretely related as possible to the congregation and the celebration involved, and that there need not be a "prayer of the faithful" in that day's liturgy, the exigency of prayer-of-the-faithful having been satisfied within the context of preparing for the eucharist in the penitential rite. An example follows, in this case for the Third Sunday of Lent:

Celebrant:	Approaching your altar in peace, we pray . . .
Response:	Lord, have mercy.
Celebrant:	Asking your forgiveness for our many sins, we pray . . .
Response:	Lord, have mercy.
Celebrant:	Asking to be renewed by participation in this holy mystery, we pray . . .
Response:	Lord, have mercy.
Celebrant:	Seeking a share in your saving death and resurrection, we pray . . .

7. **Handbook,** pp. 18f.
8. Ibid.

Response: Christ, have mercy.

Celebrant: Striving to imitate your love and sacrifice
              for all mankind, we pray . . .

Response: Christ, have mercy.

Celebrant: In the hope that our sharing in your
              holy passion may bring saving meaning
              to our own sufferings and afflictions,
              especially _____, we pray . . .[9]

Response: Christ, have mercy.

Celebrant: Asking that our efforts at prayerful
              lives of love and sacrifice during this
              holy season of Lent, in the Christian
              community of _____, may help us to
              better fulfill your will and serve the
              needs of others, we pray . . .[10]

Response: Lord, have mercy.

Celebrant: With an urgent yearning for peace throughout
              the world, especially in _____, we
              pray . . .[11]

Response: Lord, have mercy.

Celebrant: For the needs of the Church throughout

9. For instance, a hard winter, a flu epidemic in the region, general
   illness or widespread death in a particular community (e.g., when there
   are many aged and infirm among the congregation), economic difficulties
   in a certain locale, etc.
10. Here one could name either a particular parish or diocese or otherwise
    designated community. For instance, members of a town might identify
    in terms of the name of their town. Members of a parish in the Diocese
    of Brooklyn who happen to live in the County and Borough of Queens
    would almost surely not identify in terms of the name of their diocese.
    However, within a neighborhood, some parishes may have a strong
    sense of identity (e.g., St. Helena's and St. Raymond's in the northeast
    Bronx). Sometimes, it will be well to speak in terms of the whole
    metropolitan area as the community in question (e.g., "Greater New
    York", even in a parish in Union City, N.J.).
11. Obviously, an area of particular anxiety can be mentioned here, e.g.,
    the Middle East, Northern Ireland.

[134]

the world, especially ...., we pray . . .[12]

Response: Lord, have mercy.

Since it is important that such petitions in litany form
be expressed as succinctly as possible, it is almost axiomatic
that spontaneous petitions "from the floor" would not work
here, as they might in the context of the "prayer of the faithful" that would come later in most liturgies. However, it is
assumed that particular petitions from the congregation
would be fed in to the formulation of the litany in advance of
the celebration. The necessity for clear, unencumbered articulation and understanding of the petitions in the litany
seems to argue for their being spoken rather than sung, in
that the chanting of such a litany (except under virtually
ideal conditions) would tend to distract from the content
of it.

Again, this is but one example. But it is an example which
includes a number of things that should be in a penitential
rite: an acknowledgment by the worshippers of their own
sinful unworthiness and of God's saving mercy; a statement
of the central mysteries of the Faith that are to be celebrated
in the context of this particular liturgical feast or season;
supplication in terms of specific needs or exigencies in the
community in question. Like the call to worship, demonstrated above, this type of penitential rite (or one like it)
serves to alert the congregation to just what it is about in
preparing to approach the sacrificial banquet of the Lord.

12. This could be a place for mentioning the Pope and the Bishop, although it would likely suffice to remember them at the customary point
during the Eucharistic Prayer (Canon). One could here mention a
particular need of the local ecclesiastical community, i.e., the success
of a new religious-education program or mission activity, etc.

3. *A Service of the Word.*

"We have made note of the presence of Christ in the eucharistic liturgy, and of our opportunity to encounter him eucharistically," I remarked in *Transformation in Christ*,[13] "Yet, one may rightly ask, how are we to encounter Christ unless we know him, and how are we to know him? *We know him by his deeds and words as he reveals himself to us . . . in the liturgy itself.*" (emphasis added)[14] This is the function of the Service of the Word in our liturgy, to make present in a very special and salutary way the Word of God who became flesh, entering fully into the human condition in a dynamic and effective way.[15] In this light, we must understand the Service of the Word as most important to the development of true eucharistic piety for the People of God.

The Service of the Word shall have already begun, it is hoped, by way of preparation in the two liturgical stages described above, viz., the call to worship and the penitential rite. Moreover, it is to be hoped that there would be abroad in the Catholic community as a whole an ever increasing new receptivity to the Word of God in the liturgy so as to render more fertile the soil in which the seeds of revelation are to be planted.[16] This will ultimately result in greater homiletic preparation and attention, as well as greater sensitivity to Biblical themes and utterances of the teaching Church. In this context, all those involved in the preparation of a liturgical celebration—priest, lector, musicians, and the like—should work carefully and together so as to bring out the themes of a particular liturgy to best advantage. This

---

13. **Transformation in Christ**, p. 101.
14. Loc. cit.
15. Op. cit., Chapter 3, passim.
16. Mt 13:3-23; Mk 4:3-20; Lk 8:4-15.

will mean that musical expressions of worship should not be selected without reference to the Scriptural passages of the day, the themes that are likely to be developed in preaching, and so on.

Reverence for the Service of the Word in the liturgy will necessarily engender greater preparation by those who will articulate it not only in homiletic application and explanation, but also in the very announcement of it. This will mean lectors must not be selected at random, but with great care for their ability to enunciate the Biblical passages with due clarity and emphasis, all the while not falling into the traps of pretentious or stilted "dramatic reading" and similar vanities. (If I were to choose examples of the kind of thing I want to avoid, I would pick two C.B.S.-TV characters who have become popular of late: in the first regard, I would cite "Archie Bunker" on *All in the Family,* whose "dese, dem and dose" approach to the English language is sadly representative of all too many lectors and commentators today; in the second category, I would mention the pompous newscaster "Ted Baxter" on *The Mary Tyler Moore Show.*)

Of course, in the rediscovery of the importance of the Service of the Word, there will be more than simply the proclamation of the Word itself. There will also be a response, ultimately in deed, but at first in liturgical prayer. Here, we would make a tragic mistake if we disregarded the responses to the Scriptures in the liturgy as one more thing to be "recited". The responses to the Biblical passages in the eucharistic liturgy should be as deliberate, and as emphatic, as possible. My own suggestion for this is that at least the *Alleluia* of the Gospel Acclamation be sung. This can be done antiphonally, with the congregation singing any one of a number of simple *Alleluia* melodies (e.g., the triple *Alleluia* from Gelineau's Psalms 92 and 99,[17] or from

17. Joseph Gelineau, **Twenty-four Psalms and a Canticle** (Toledo, Ohio:

the traditional hymn *O Filii et Filiae*,[18] or from the Easter Vigil service,[19] or one of Fitzpatrick's *Alleluia* settings)[20] while the changeable verses of the Acclamation are sung by a cantor or choir (even an inexperienced cantor or choir can sing *recto tono* or one of the simple Gregorian psalm-tones, e.g., 8g; of course, some more creative and interesting things can be done).

The Response to the First Reading can be said (I am wary of the word *recited*, implying mechanical response, but will tolerate its use once I have explained my caveat), preferably in antiphonal fashion between leader and congregation (as indicated in most "pew books", e.g., Paluch's Monthly *Missalette*).[21] More elaborate versions would have the congregation divide (e.g., into sides of the nave) for alternate speaking of the parts of the response, and so on. Of course, the Response could be sung, using a simple refrain by the congregation (from Gunther, Gelineau, Deiss, Fitzpatrick, Somerville, or whomever) and verses by the *schola* or cantor. Finally, there are times when the solemnity of the response to the Word of God in the liturgy could be enhanced by a sung response done by a choir alone (one thinks, in this connection, of some of the shorter pieces of Ravanello, and wonders if there could not be a vernacular selection of similar appropriateness for some of our liturgies today).

Gregorian Institute of America), trans. Clifford Howell and Gregory Murray. This is the 1955 American release, subsequent to the English release by the Ladies of the Grail.

18. Benedictines of Solesmes, comp., **Liber Usualis** (Tournai: Desclee & Co., 1952).
19. Ibid.
20. Dennis Fitzpatrick, ed., **The English Liturgy Hymnal** (Chicago: F.E.L. Publishing Company, 1965).
21. Published by J. S. Paluch Co., Chicago, Illinois. Some numbers of the **Missalette** are now seasonal (e.g., Advent) rather than simply "monthly".

In any case, I would want to stress the point that the mode of response would best enjoy some variety, albeit within a context of some identifiable consistency or coherence, so that even the most solemnly-expressed response will not be in danger of becoming insipid. Also, I would insist that the content of the response is always central, and the mode of the response is always less important, since it is but a means to the end of involving the People of God in responding prayerfully to the Word in their midst. While there will necessarily be a response to this Word in the prayer of the Church at formal worship, there will—or should—ultimately be a greater response in terms of the lives of the members of the Christian community in response to the living Word of God made present in the ongoing vitality of the teaching Church as Christ in the world. For this reason, there is a great deal of re-emphasis—most rightly so!—on the sermon or homily.

The term *homily* is more than a fashionable piece of post-Conciliar nomenclature, although it often comes to be used interchangeably (and sometimes indiscriminately) with the word *sermon*. Actually, sermon denotes preaching in general, while homily refers specifically to some explanation and/or application of the Biblical themes in a particular liturgy. All homilies can be called sermons; not all sermons can be called homilies. In recent liturgical opinion, it has become popular to disdain the designation *sermon* and opt for the term *homily,* and concomitantly to advocate the utilization of a homily, strictly speaking, on each occasion when preaching takes place in a liturgical context.[22] While

22. Cf. **Lectionary for Mass,** from The Roman Missal, revised by decree of the Second Vatican Council and published by authority of Pope Paul VI, English Translation approved by the National Conference of Catholic Bishops and confirmed by the Apostolic See (New York: Catholic Book Publishing Company, 1970), pp. 5f.

this emphasis is laudable in the main, it must be understood within a particular historical context: up until at least the era of the Vatican Council II (1962-65), Catholic preaching was in a state of disrepute. Pastors often felt that the real presence of Jesus in the eucharist made it unnecessary to attract congregations by what they considered oratorical gimmicks.[23] Thus sermons in Catholic churches were at best lacklustre on the whole, and often tended to be fund-raising harangues or disjointed lectures on the preacher's pet subject.[24] It is against this background that the Church in recent years has insisted that preaching in the context of the eucharistic celebration be geared to the particular feast being celebrated, i.e., the Biblical passages pertinent to that specific liturgy. In this connection I would submit that the foregoing would be an excellent norm against which to measure preaching, but that it need not be implemented slavishly or legalistically. There may well be good reason to digress from the Biblical or liturgical theme of a particular celebration in a given instance, provided that the overall homiletic effort in that community is consonant with the above norms, and provided also that the digression is not for the sort of purposes condemned before (e.g., a fund-raising talk about a particular project, which really is not fit matter for the pulpit in the liturgy).[25]

One point also being made with regard to preaching nowadays is that shorter sermons are apt to be the more effective ones, in that the interest or attention span of the average congregation is apt not to tolerate or digest a sermon of more than about seven minutes. This is not hard to imagine, in an age when so many of our television stories

23. Wills, **Bare Ruined Choirs**, p. 68.
24. Cf. **Transformation in Christ**, chap. 5, p. 12.
25. Ibid.

are initiated, exposed, complicated and concluded within the space of twenty-six minutes (allowing time for commercials), and the most popular newspaper in the United States is heavily laden with photographs, easy on the words, and able to be read quickly on the subway in the morning.[26] Over a decade ago, the great liturgist and preacher Frank B. Norris, speaking of liturgical preaching,[27] said that no sermon should exceed seven minutes, and that he always tried to finish within five, so that even if he went a bit over, he would still be within the seven-minute maximum. This is probably better for the communication of a message to a community than the approach which strives for a lengthier exposition in the hope that all the subtle nuances will somehow get across (they seldom do; people tend to think in rather unsubtle terms on the whole).[28] This will force preachers to strive for economy and precision in the words and expressions they choose; the task will be far from easy, but its pursuit should serve well the Christian community as a whole. And many a priest will find that his ministry in an age of the renewed liturgy of the Church will be increasingly a ministry of the word.[29]

Of course, the remarks above have to do essentially with the conventional homiletic situation in which the preacher preaches and the congregation listens to him. What about some experimental or contemporary approaches to the service of the word which have enjoyed some currency of late, viz., the dialogue homily and the multimedia homily? It

26. The New York Daily News.
27. At a special summer institute I attended, "Worship and the Word", at the College of Notre Dame, Belmont, California, 1960.
28. For this reason, the sermon materials in If I Were to Preach tend to be shorter in the beginning of the liturgical year, then become longer.
29. In this context, sermon-aid materials like If I Were to Preach are no substitute (nor are they meant to be) for the role of the individual homilist.

should be acknowledged at the outset that these can be of great value to the worshipping community, provided they are used judiciously and not simply as "gimmicks", and provided also that certain specific considerations are taken into account, which may lead to their acceptance by the Church.

With regard to the "dialogue" homily, it must be pointed out that there can be no dialogue unless parties are prepared to take part in conversation of a somewhat substantial sort from more than one side. I have more than once been a party to the "dialogue" homily introduced by an *avant-garde* priest to an unprepared (albeit not hostile) congregation (especially in school liturgies, informal home Masses, and the like), wherein the priest's attempts at informality and "let's get everyone into this" only serve to increase the sense of general discomfort in the situation. What I have often witnessed, following the reading of the Gospel, has been something like this: the priest sits down (sometimes at the *sedilia,* sometimes—hiking up his chasuble—on the lowest step of the altar, sometimes Indian-style on the floor) and says something chummy like, "Hi, my name is John! What did you think of the Gospel we just read?" That the congregation should gape in silence should be no surprise at all. The priest, despite all his attempts (presumably most sincere) at creating a relaxed atmosphere, has not created an atmosphere of *preparation*. To partake in any sort of "dialogue" homily, members of the congregation should have read the Biblical passages for the celebration ahead of time (as should the preacher or celebrating priest) and hopefully even some learned commentary on them, and meditated on their implications to some extent. In this way, people will have something to say. When they *don't* have anything to say (which is usually the case, unhappily), they fulfill the physical minima of vocal participation in the "dialogue" by mouthing some sort of fashionable theological truism ("Today's Gospel tells us that we must love and be open to one another", etc.) which takes no account of the specific liturgy which the Church has constructed for the edification of its members.

In a word, I feel rather strongly that the "dialogue homily" is a technique which the Church should permit only in congregations that are somewhat specially prepared for it, not only because someone thinks they are intellectually well-disposed to it, but because they actually can and do prepare (in this light, a group of people who never attended college could be more thoroughly prepared than a group of graduate students . . . in fact, the odds are that the latter group might consider themselves too well-versed to bother preparing). This sort of preparation can be successful, I further submit, only in a congregation whose membership is not unmanageably large (not necessarily the Biblical twelve, but surely not more than a couple of hundred at the outside)[30] and is somewhat stable (so that its members have some notion of the degree and kind of preparation that would be expected of them).

Another condition for the success of a "dialogue" homily, I feel, is some pre-arranged suspension of the time limitations normally prevalent for the eucharistic liturgy. This would mean a Service of the Word which might be as long as an hour or more in length (possibly becoming the time for such functions in a congregation as a Biblical study group, social-problems discussion group, etc.) in a Mass whose total duration might approach the two- or three-hour mark. It would immediately be apparent that not everyone would be attracted to this type of situation, and that factor in itself should serve to limit the numbers of participants. Further-

30. This figure presumes only **representative** participation, not that of each individual vocally.

more, the regular obligations to worship (cf. Chapter 4, supra) might well be interpreted more flexibly (say, every *other* week) in the instance of a liturgical celebration which, including the Service of the Word, would be more intensive than the typical Mass. This would only be possible in the event of a change in the Church's prevailing discipline, which in itself is unlikely unless some of the concerns I have mentioned here are taken into account.

Finally, as many liturgical authorities[31] have pointed out, any "dialogue" homily is never a substitute for or diminution of the responsibility and authoritative function of the preacher, who remains charged with the education of the congregation in the Service of the Word. This means, concretely, that from initiation through participation until conclusion, any "dialogue" homily would still be the responsibility of the preacher who prepares for it, initiates it, supervises it, directs it, leads it, keeps it from going off onto unproductive tangents, and coordinates its conclusion to a concrete awareness (however rudimentary) of the presence and meaning of the revealed Word of God amidst the Christian community in a way that is somehow greater than it was before the homily began.

With regard to "multimedia" homilies (i.e., utilizing films, sound recordings or the like) I would make all of the same observations: the congregation must be specially prepared for this type of approach, including an adjustment of time limitations, and the homilist himself must be specifically and thoroughly responsible for the conduct of the Service of the Word in such wise as to achieve its ends, whether by conventional or contemporary/experimental

31. E.g., Msgr. John Koenig, head of the liturgical commission of the Archdiocese of Newark and a professor of liturgies at Immaculate Conception Seminary, Darlington, N.J., in a meeting I attended at Caldwell College, Caldwell, N.J., in January, 1969.

An Agonizing Reappraisal

means. To illustrate briefly: Imagine that the decision has been made to utilize a short film that runs 15 minutes, and to discuss thereafter its implications. It is obvious that, in addition to possessing the technical competence necessary to bring off the showing of the film (what can be more exasperating than a poor sound system, a broken film or an unreliable projector?) the preacher or the coordinator for the presentation should ensure that there will exist the right atmosphere for the viewing of the film (alternately, the hearing of the recording, or whatever the case may be), including adequate time and receptivity on the part of the congregation for both the presentation and the appropriate response to it. Finally, we should reiterate the notion that "new" means of homiletic presentation should never be utilized as "gimmicks", i.e., must always draw attention to the Word and never to themselves alone. Only if such conditions are met can liturgists hope to see the Church come to allow such practices.

The same is true, incidentally, with regard to what has come to be called "extra-Scriptural" or "extra-Biblical" material within the Service of the Word for purposes of articulating the liturgical themes of the day. I have often been asked my opinion as to the substitution of thematic material from modern literature, cinema, music, etc., for one or more of the Scriptural readings in the liturgical service, and my response is that such material may enhance the Biblical material of the liturgy by being added to it, but not by being substituted for it (which is not allowed by the liturgical instructions of the Church). There exists in today's liturgy enough opportunity to substitute a variety of materials (including modern songs, poems set to music, etc.) for the proper parts of the Mass (Entrance hymn, etc.) so that this need for the expression of an individual community in contemporary terms in a specific

[145]

cultural situation is not being ignored. There is also a need for coherence within the total context of a worshipping community larger than the particular congregation. To this we are called by the Word of God in the Scriptures of the liturgy (replete with alternative choices provided in the Lectionary)[32] that we may worship with a view to a constancy of revelation and ecclesial identity. It would be a shame indeed to disrupt the balance that we have achieved in this regard, and should we not work with and in relation to the Scriptural materials of the liturgy, rather than in spite of them?

4. *A Eucharistic Sacrifice and Banquet.*

The very words I have chosen to head this section should make clear my belief that the eucharistic liturgy (despite some of the theological polemics that have been visited upon the Church of late) is both sacrifice and banquet.[33] If there was difficulty understanding the complementary nature of these elements in the liturgy, then much has been done to improve the situation in the *Ordo Missae* of 1970, which has made the Offertory Rite more concise and consistent, and allowed for the use of Eucharistic Prayers (Canons) beyond simply the Roman Canon (Eucharistic Prayer I in today's enumeration) which is in part a repository of Gallican accretions.[34] However, I submit, even within the framework of new optionality and flexibility, we must take care that we take best advantage of our new liturgical opportunities.

For over a decade, offertory processions have been gaining popularity in Catholic churches. The new offertory rite is no less conducive than its predecessor to this practice. In-

---

32. Cf. **Lectionary for Mass**, loc. cit.
33. Cf. **Transformation in Christ**, Chapter 5.
34. **Handbook**, pp. 26-28.

deed, the ability to eschew a spoken offertory prayer in favor
of an appropriate sung prayer for the offertory procession is
somewhat an improvement over the prior dispensation, provided the sung response is chosen judiciously and is thus
suitable either to the offertory action or to the feast being
celebrated. While it is common for offertory processions to
involve a token representation of the total congregation (in
some cases, the communicants of the congregation having
put their hosts into the ciborium at an "offertory table"
before Mass), we should not disregard altogether the possibility of involving the whole congregation in the offertory
procession when the congregation is manageably small (no
more than, say, a couple of hundred), there is no real pressure to "get 'em in and get 'em out" (as usually prevails in
large parishes on Sundays and holydays), and there can be
an appropriate sung prayer (e.g., an antiphonal response
for the congregation to a psalm sung chorally or by a cantor). For some special occasions, this might be a fitting
emphasis of the role of the entire worshipping community
in the action of the Mass, especially the offertory. However,
it is evident that this could be done only in a limited number
of situations.

When the more common type of offertory procession
(i.e., a representative procession) is used, care should be
taken to see that the offertory procession (generally, not
necessarily in one particular instance) reflects the make-up
of the total worshipping community as to age, gender, racial
or ethnic background, etc. (When I have arranged offertory
or other liturgical processions representative of the congregation for Masses at Seton Hall University, I have tried to
somehow represent men, women, students, faculty, staff
administrators, undergraduates, graduates, the four undergraduate schools, the South Orange, Paterson and Newark

campuses, etc.; needless to say, not all of these could be represented at once, but I think an attempt should be made along those lines.)

If the congregation is to participate in a song at the offertory, it is again important to do something along the lines we spoke of for a "call to worship" in the entrance rite, above. Remember, congregational participation in worship-music is either an important part of the liturgical action or else an irrelevant accompaniment to it. If it is indeed the former, let us treat it as such in introducing and executing it; if not, forget it. Thus the congregation's involvement in the offertory song or psalm should be initiated by a "call to worship" motivated in terms of the action of the offertory, e.g., "As our representatives bring to the altar our gifts for the sacrificial banquet of the Mass, let us sing our offertory song in the hymnal at number . . .", or "Our representatives, today chosen from the eighth grade of our parish school, are bringing to Father the gifts we offer as signs of ourselves in the Mass. Let us proclaim the meaning of this by singing our offertory psalm, number . . .", or whatever. Even in the absence of a song, the same type of "motivation" should be apparent in a "call to worship", rather than a mere announcement ("Off'tory—sen'teen-oh'two!"), a timid request ("Would you please all join in . . .") or the initiation of a schoolroom exercise ("Let us now recite together . . ."). The same principle will apply not only to the entrance and offertory procession, but to communion, to any recessional hymn, to spoken and sung responses and other congregational parts of the liturgy.

We should note, too, that the new offertory rite, far less cumbersome and out of proportion to the Canon than the one used before the 1970 *Ordo Missae,* is a fitting statement of the meaning of the action involved and allows for a most appropriate congregational response in spoken prayer.

This should not be disdained as "not enough" for the offertory, and can often be chosen as a meaningful way of involving a worshipping community in the liturgical action and meaning of the offertory rite. While a certain stability of custom is helpful to community worship, it should be taken into account that some alternation of options is healthy so as to prevent stagnation, both in the offertory rite and other parts of the liturgy where options are available.

The same principle, I believe, should be applied to the Eucharistic Prayer, known to many of us by its more traditional name, the Canon of the Mass. Liturgical scholars have pointed out how we have had more than one "Canon" in the history of the Church, even within the Roman Rite as it has come to us today. Furthermore, the most familiar Canon (the Roman Canon, known nowadays as Eucharistic Prayer I) came to be a rather unwieldy amalgam of the Roman Canon and numerous accretions from the Gallican rite, with its many prayers of supplication, enumerations of saints (*Communicantes . . .; Nobis quoque peccatoribus . . .*) and so forth.[35] As a result of recent liturgical scholarship, then, we now have four Eucharistic Prayers from which to choose in our rite (the first being the form known as the Roman Canon).

Everyone is likely to have his own preference among these options: some admire the simplicity of Eucharistic Prayer III; others the theological richness of Number IV; some (even appreciating its difficulties) are drawn to the traditional phrases of the "old Roman Canon", Number I. Preferences like these are eminently understandable and legitimate among celebrants and laity alike. The important point, though, is that the Church provides options because the Church wishes the options to be used to full advantage.

35. Cf. Cipriano Vaggagini, **The Canon of the Mass and Liturgical Reform** (Staten Island, N.Y.: Alba House, 1967), tr. ed. Peter Coughlan; Jungmann, **The Mass of the Roman Rite**, pp. 402ff., 446ff.

Thus it would be a real abuse of the freedom afforded since the 1970 promulgation of the *Ordo* to consistently elect only the shortest Eucharistic Prayer, or the Roman Canon for its "traditional" flavor, or whichever one appeals to us personally as a favorite. Care should be taken to select for every liturgical celebration the Canon or Eucharistic Prayer which is likely to be most appropriate to the feast and the circumstances. (In some cases, practical situations may call for brevity, but this should not be a permanently overriding factor in making a choice.) The same will be true with responses to the eucharistic acclamation. It would be a real shame to always choose the response "Christ has died; Christ is risen; Christ will come again!"[36] simply because it was promulgated to and learned by most American Catholic congregations before the alternative responses.

There is among American Catholics, I fear, a tendency to be almost sinfully unimaginative or uncreative, to be excessively docile and passive whenever the specter of choice appears to be present. For how many years did most congregations sing *O Salutaris Hostia* at Benediction believing it was required (actually, any eucharistic hymn would have done)? Likewise, how many thought "Holy God, We Praise Thy Name" was written into the rubrics at Rome itself? Our tendency, all too often, is to take the most familiar option and make it tantamount to an irreversible mandate from the deity. This is exactly the sort of thing which leads to stagnation, and to a deadening of our sensibilities in liturgical worship. And this is just the sort of thing the Church wants to avoid; hence, the Church provides options so that we may use them wisely and regularly.

This will mean that care must be taken, again, with regard to eucharistic-acclamation responses (as with Canons, penitential rites, ways of participating in the offertory, etc.)

36. **Handbook,** loc. cit.

so as to select the option most meaningful and most appropriate to this celebration, of this feast, in this assembly, at
this time, in this particular place. To take such care is to
increase the likelihood that our congregations will be united
in the action of the eucharistic liturgy, and the *Amen* which
concludes the Eucharistic Prayer as the ratification of the
entire People of God.

The reform of the Roman liturgy has returned to proper
proportion the elevation of the consecrated Species and the
concluding *Amen*—or "Great *Amen*"—at the end of the
Eucharistic Prayer. No more do we hear people refer to
the latter as "the *minor* elevation", as they generally did a
decade ago.[37] Beyond the emphasis given the "great *Amen*"
by the reform of the liturgy, it has become popular in some
congregations to proclaim this affirmation in song rather than
to speak it. My own experience with it is that American
Catholics tend to regard a sung *Amen* as a bit artificial; we
have just gotten them used to singing a hymn or antiphon,
but singing a word they are accustomed to speaking is quite
another matter.[38] I would say that where the practice seems
to be helpful for the meaningful involvement of the congregation in the liturgy, it should doubtless be continued, but
elsewhere, attempting it would likely divert time, attention
and energy from liturgical priorities of a weightier sort.

The same sort of artificiality threatens to ruin attempts
at congregational involvement in the *pax* or peace ceremony,
since its wholesale restoration in the wake of the 1970 *Ordo
Missae*.[39] Again taking the modern American experience and
character into account, it should be acknowledged that we

37. A few liturgical **cognoscenti** dissented from this common nomenclature,
    but this was hardly more than an exception to prove the rule.
38. As Dennis Fitzpatrick has pointed out in his **English Liturgy Hymnal**.
    and related materials, q.v., the singing of "Ayyyy-mennn" is at best
    jarring to the liturgical and musical ear. Nowadays, the singing of "Ah-
    men" is hard to carry off, with a people used to saying "Ay-men".
39. **Handbook**, loc. cit.

are not, as a rule, a very expressive people. We listen to someone else sing the national anthem at ball games, we watch the heroics of others on the gridiron, we read about or view on the screen the adventurous lives of people whom we would like to emulate (but generally do not); even the popularity of pornography indicates that Americans sin against sexual purity more often in thought and word than in deed. This is not to suggest that we do not have strong emotions or drives, simply that we are not apt to express them easily in overt ways, especially in public or among "strangers". This is why, when our celebrant tells us to greet our "neighbors" in church with a gesture of fraternal well-wishing, our best response is usually a cold-fish hand-shake and the mechanical versicle and response, "Peace be with you/and with you too", or the like.

Part of the problem, of course, is our reluctance to be ex-pressive (particularly if our ethnic background is Irish, as in the case of many American Catholics). It is this sort of reluctance that manifests itself in raised eyebrows if my wife and I, at the proper time during Mass, express this "peace greeting" to each other with the sort of kiss that would never have violated the norms laid down for a modest expression of affection among adolescent daters in the old pamphlet *Modern Youth and Chastity*.[40] It is this sort of reluctance, too, that makes people signal by their expressions and postures the fact that they will not physically resist a handclasp or greeting, but that they are not looking forward to one either. A lot of time and experience has to melt that reluctance to express fraternity and charity to a neighbor in the Christian community.

But something else has to happen, too. We must work to improve the very situations that *make* us strangers to

40. George A. Kelly, **Modern Youth and Chastity** (St. Louis: The Queen's Work, 1943).

our fellow worshippers. This is becoming increasingly important in a society of urban communities becoming more mobile by the day. More and more, our territorial parishes are coming to contain people whose only common identity is in terms of where they sleep and vote. Mobility, both of necessity and by choice, has brought about situations where people commonly recreate, work, shop, and pursue a host of other activities in places other than the localities where they "live". To deal with this realistically means to do any or all of the following: cultivate more "parishes" or worshipping communities constructed on criteria which make more sense than mere geography (cf. Chapter 4, supra); make worshipping communities—or at least "sub-parishes" as small as reasonably possible so as to create a sense of identity in community; in large and disconnected worshipping communities that do not admit of much change, *do all possible to make members neighbors and no longer strangers.*

There are various ways in which worshipping communities will seek to make true neighbors of their members even without change in the parochial structures we now know. But in any event, we must see to it that we do all we can to make of our congregations true communities of faith, hope and charity and not merely aggregations of people who happen to be in the same location at the same time for the same series of identical individual purposes (as in a bus queue). This will be necessary not only to make meaningful the *pax* or greeting of peace in our liturgy, but to do likewise for the whole of the eucharistic banquet, a feast of charity in Christ which is unworthy of praise if it is untrue to its meaning.[41]

The same will be true of the communion procession, of

41. Cf. I Cor 10.

course, in that partaking of the eucharist is not only the supreme sign of our thanksgiving *(eucharistia)* for Christ's redemptive presence, but also the communal celebration of our fraternal charity in the Lord. This will mean, in addition, that the liturgical procession for the partaking of the congregation in the eucharistic banquet must proclaim the meaning of the action as forcefully and clearly as possible. In this regard, I must mention again (as in Chapter 5, supra) the desirability of antiphonal singing during this part of the Mass. The difficulties of involving a congregation in singing are legendary, especially at a time when people are accustomed to some private meditation and are also involved in the physical movement of a communion procession. However, if these difficulties cannot be eliminated, they can surely be minimized by proper forethought for the congregation's participation in sung worship during communion. I have in mind here the kinds of communion antiphons which a congregation can sing with relative ease, requiring no hymnals or whatever, while a choir or cantor sings the verses in between (e.g., Fitzpatrick's "Where There Is Charity And Love" based on the *Ubi Caritas;* many of the Gelineau and Somerville psalms, some of Father Deiss' antiphons, some folk-Mass pieces, and some of the works of composers who as yet are lesser-known, like Malcolm Williamson). Some hymns can be adapted for antiphonal singing as well, like some English versions of *Adoro Te Devote* ("Humbly We Adore Thee"), providing they keep a common refrain at the end of each verse for the congregation (the early editions of *Peoples Mass Book*[42] did not do this, and went so far as to print the confusing hymn on three consecutive pages of the hymnal; one can imagine the chore of singing that during a communion procession, when it *could* have been so simple!).

42. Cincinnati, Ohio: World Library of Sacred Music, 1965.

Finally, after communion there should be some opportunity for meditation on the day's liturgy, which has just culminated in reception of the eucharist, and which will radiate into daily lives of Christian witness in the *saeculum*.[43] If feasible, a choral selection or instrumental interlude can be appropriate for facilitating meditation at this time, and this can provide an opportunity to perform some fine works of liturgical music whose role has been considered "diminished" in the wake of vernacularization and *aggiornamento* in the liturgy since Vatican II.

5. A Thanksgiving-and-dismissal Rite.

The meditation period after communion, in a way, telescopes into this final portion of the liturgical celebration. If it is desired to make a particular point of emphasis for a specific liturgical occasion, it would not be out of order for one of the leaders of the worship-action of the community to have either begun or concluded the meditation time with a brief statement of the theme in question as it pertains to the liturgy and to the lives to be led as outgrowths of the liturgical assembly. For example, something like this could be said for the Feast of the Holy Family: "As we conclude our celebration of the Feast of the Holy Family, let us think of ways in which each of us can make our own family lives mirrors of the love that should be obvious in the world, especially among those of us who dare to be called followers of Jesus Christ." Such commentary should not be overbearing, or long, and it probably should not be a regular thing, but the occasional use of such a technique—even frequently—can serve as one more connection between liturgy and life in general.

It is on that note, connection between liturgy and life

43. **Saeculum** in the sense of here-and-now; cf. **Transformation in Christ,** loc. cit.

in general, that our celebrations should begin, proceed and conclude. So it will be that the final prayers, the blessing and dismissal of the People of God, and their final proclamation of worship in a majestic (albeit simple) song of praise and dedication should serve to confirm in their own hearts and as a dynamic presence in the world the saving love of the Word who fully entered and now constantly redeems the human condition. To strive for this is not to "let the liturgy take care of itself", as was too long and too often the case in the past. If celebrations of the eucharistic liturgy are lacklustre, meaningless and agonizing, it is because they have been left to take care of themselves, once the minimal requirements of Church law and rubrics are satisfied. But if celebrations of the Mass, the primary religious action and experience of Catholics, are to be sources of true leaven within the one bread which is the one Body of Christ, then it will be only because intelligent, sensitive, dedicated, skilled members of the worshipping People of God have worked for that end, and for the radiation of our liturgical worship into lives which make the Risen Lord dynamically and redemptively present in the world.

CHAPTER SEVEN

Renewal in the Reconciliation Liturgy

MODERN CATHOLICS are beginning to rediscover the Sacrament of Penance under a more appropriate name, the "Sacrament of Reconciliation". In this chapter, we shall endeavor to investigate this sacrament as one which reconciles the sinner who has cut himself off from the eucharistic community by his rejection of God's love.

Even within this century, popular treatments and notions of the Sacrament of Reconciliation—if they have not obscured this notion—have not allowed such an understanding to be made clearly manifest. One can see this in terms of some existing practices in the penitential ritual of the Roman Rite, as well as in terms of the catechetical background which has been bound up with these practices. In short, our understanding of this sacrament has been hampered by a ritual situation and a theological expression which have both been somewhat less than perfect.

Let us examine the Sacrament of Reconciliation in these aspects: first, the background of the Old Testament, in which we can see some evidence for a notion of sin and atonement as communal or *ecclesial* realities; second, some theological basis for this in the witness of the New Testament; third, a brief examination of the Church's earlier penitential rituals, which underscore the concept of the Sacrament of Penance as the Sacrament of Reconciliation; fourth, a survey of the present ritual, insofar as it does and/or does not convey that concept; finally, let us consider some suggestions as to how the celebration of this sacrament can be more significant (viz. more *sacramental*), in terms of the concrete situation of our own age.

[157]

Strictly speaking, it could be said that our primary consideration here will be with the penitential ritual as such (the *sacramentum* of Penance, if you will). This is not to say that the "what" or "how" of the sacrament will eclipse consideration of the "why" (for this reason we do not say *sacramentum tantum*), but since sacraments are *signs* of salvation, our considerations of the theology of the sacrament will be centered in the liturgy which communicates that theology.

It should be added, too, that our main considerations will be centered on reconciliation following a serious rejection of God's love, *i.e.*, mortal sin, since in this manner we may clearly focus on the main function of the sacrament. This is not to say that the concept of venial sin will be discarded here, but that it will not be a major consideration for our purposes.[1]

1. The Old Testament.

In beginning our considerations of Old Testament background, we might remark as to their significance. The question might be asked, "What has the Old Testament—or more clearly, the pre-Christian era of Salvation-History—to do with the distinctively Christian reality which is the Sacrament of Penance?" Here, of course, we must remind the reader that the revelation and establishment of the New Covenant simply did not take place in a theological or historical vacuum (as was hopefully made clear in earlier chapters). Even a general acquaintance with the Old Testament would seem to lead one to the necessary conclusion that the com-

1. As will become evident in this chapter, the emphasis on the early Church was on grave sin with regard to the Sacrament of Penance, and emphasis on venial sins developed later. Cf. **CIC**, Can. 906, and Suso Mayer, "Devotional Confession", **Orate, Fratres**, XVIII (1944), pp. 15ff.

munication of the New Testament revelation in Christ was not *ex nihilo,* but that it drew on the gradually maturing religious awareness of the pre-Christian *Qahal Yahweh.* This is especially important in terms of the sacraments of the New Covenant, in that all of them involve natural symbols already present. This is rather obvious in some cases (e.g., Baptism, the Eucharist), but may be least clear in the case of the ritual expression of the Sacrament of Penance.

Here, then, we will briefly examine some evidence which conveys the notion of sin and reconciliation as communal realities in the Old Testament. Within the framework of scholastic theology, we would refer to the "matter" of a sacrament as the physical element specified by God's Word (*e.g.,* water, bread, oil, *etc.*).[2] In Penance, the "matter", or in more familiar terms, that already-present human experience which Christ chooses as a sign of his saving activity, would traditionally be considered to be three "acts" of the penitent: contrition of heart, confession and penance for sins (actually called *quasi-materia,* in technical language, because not corporeal).[3] Here I would hasten to add that an ironclad enumeration of "three acts of the penitent" as such will not apply univocally to our considerations of the Old Testament period, which antedates this formal enumeration by many centuries. However, we hope to see in our analysis that same reality which we may simply refer to as the "penitential situation" of the member of the community, which would *de facto*—if not *de jure*—involve the "three acts" of later formulation.

2. Bernard Leeming, **Principles of Sacramental Theology** (Westminster, Md.: Newman Press, 1960), pp. 403-407.
3. Loc. cit. Also cf. F. De Letter, "Two Concepts of Attrition and Contrition", TS, XI (March, 1950), pp. 3-33; DS 1323, 1673-5, 914. Finally, cf. Gerald Pire, "The **Res et Sacramentum** in Four Contemporary Theologians" (Milwaukee, Wis.: unpublished thesis, Marquette University, 1968).

If we are to consider the "penitential situation" in the Old Testament, it is necessary to keep in mind the consciousness Israel had of herself as a *people*, not just a group of individuals, but a corporate entity.[4] And sin, for Israel, is a community matter, as seen by Henri Rondet:

> Among the Jews, the sinner-type is Israel itself, sometimes the friend and sometimes the enemy of God. It is the people who turn away from Yahweh or who return in a spirit of repentance. The Law is given to the people; it is the entire nation that suffers when the violations of this Law accumulate. Sin and its punishment, its expiation and redemption, all of this has a powerfully marked social character. When the prophets place emphasis on individual responsibility, they merely underline the guilt of each individual member of a sinful community . . .[5]

While Israel had its individual trespass or guilt offerings as repentance rites (cf. II Kings 12:16; Esdras 40:39; Leviticus 5:14-26; 7:1-6), it is important to note those corporate sin offerings occasioned by the sin of the people as a whole, or by the high priest, whose sin brought guilt upon the whole people (cf. Leviticus 4:1-5:13; 6:17-23), and of course the annual Day of Atonement *(Yom Kippur)*, a ritual consecration by the high priest of the entire nation of Israel, similar to the sin offering in ritual (cf. Leviticus 16; 23:27-32; Numbers 29:7-11).[6]

It is also important to point out that, while Israel stressed sin and repentance (as well as punishment) as corporate,

4. Myriad references could be cited here concerning the establishment of Israel as Yahweh's people (Qahal 'Yahweh) by covenant, e.g., Gn 17; Ex 19-24; and the prophetic conscience of Israel as people—e.g., Ez 36:23-28. Also note Israel's awareness of this in the Psalms.
5. Henri Rondet, **The Theology of Sin** (Notre Dame, Ind.: Fides Press, 1960), pp. 12-13.
6. Cf. Roland deVaux, **Ancient Israel** (New York: McGraw-Hill, 1961), pp. 419ff; George F. Moore, **Judaism** (Cambridge, Mass.: Harvard University Press, 1962), Vol. I, pp. 460-507; Gottfried Quell, et al., "Sin", in **Bible Key Words** (New York: Harper and Brothers, 1951). (E. T. of Gerhard Kittel, **Theologisches Worterbuch zum Neuen Testament**, tr. and ed. J. R. Coates.)

the individual Jew marred by sin could not participate in the liturgy with the rest of the worshipping community until he had been purified.[7]

The emphases to be found on corporate *and* personal responsibility for sin in the Old Testament might at first appear to be, if not contradictory, at least puzzling in the light of each other. Here we must take into account the fact that God, as his revealed plan of working with his people shows, deals with man "as is", i.e., man is an individual, yet is a social being: he functions within a community (and often, when unable to function, it is for lack of a community in which to do so); at the same time, while he and his feelings and actions are part of a communal situation, he is still personally responsible for them. While the notions of corporate and individual responsibility are really aspects of one integral reality, they can, on the conceptual level, appear to set up a dialectic. Rondet notes that

> These (ideas stressing corporate responsibility) allow us to draw closer to the mystery of original sin, but we run the risk of neglecting personal responsibility. And when sociology and depth psychology tell us that our environment determines our acts, the concept of formal sin is completely lost.[8]

I think Rondet overstates the case, but let us consider the relationship between individual and community in a manner that is *complementary*: while an individual is within a community, it is his individuality which allows him to become a member of a community: take away individual personality, and you do not have community.

The Old Testament "penitential situation", then, can be said to include a notion of Israel related to God precisely as a *people,* and thus of sin and atonement as communal or

7. Johs. Pedersen, **Israel** (Copenhagen: Dyva & Jeppesen, 1940), pp. 359-364.
8. Henri Rondet, "Towards a Theology of Sin", TD IV (Autumn, 1956), p. 173.

ecclesial realities, wherein the worshipping community must be purified in order to encounter her divine Friend and Benefactor, Yahweh; so must be purified—so must be responsible—the individual members of the community. And let us not say that the "penitential situation" ceases with a ritual purification, since it involves purification by penance as well (cf. Hosea 11:7).

Our considerations, however brief, of the Old Testament "penitential situation", establish some background for—and lead us to discussion of—that "penitential situation" which is to prevail in the New Covenant.

2. The New Testament.

If the Old Testament gives seed to the notion of sin and atonement as corporate realities, then does the New Testament bring this concept to fruition. In the pre-Christian era, the People of God present themselves to Yahweh in terms of their adherence to the Law. In the New Testament, the same is basically true, but the law is clearer, even in its lack of specific precepts. To cite Rondet again: "It would be futile to search the Gospel for a systematic catalogue of virtues to practice or of sins to avoid. The supreme rule of moral life is Charity (Mt 22:37-40); we will be judged by our attitude towards our neighbor (Mt 25:31-46). Thus, the New Law is extremely simple, but it is very exacting."[9] While it is true that Jesus addressed himself to a variety of topical questions during his earthly ministry, there remained numerous moral difficulties in the practical order which were not anticipated, in his moral prescriptions to his followers. It would remain for the teaching Church to explicate the demands of the Christian message, sometimes with certainty that a particular teaching came from the Lord, and sometimes by offering a tenta-

9. The Theology of Sin, p. 27.

tive solution to a specific moral dilemma at a particular time.[10]

Christ in the New Testament establishes a community which by its nature is directed to lead *towards* community, i.e., a society in time whose purpose is a unity which transcends temporal limitations, a unity through him with the Father, in the Holy Spirit, and of Christians with one another, to enjoy with Jesus divine sonship, to be united with him in such a way as to share in his redemptive passion-death-resurrection-ascension to the Father. Christ, in sharing with us divine sonship, redeems man not only individually but in a corporate context, and establishes that "corporation" (in the strict sense of the term) which makes possible human sharing in his dying to sin and rising to grace. In making his followers one body (Rm 12:5; I Cor 12:13) he does so that he might reconcile all (Eph 2:16) in one body regardless of social, racial or other distinctions. That unity to which Christ draws men is the unity of love. The law to which he binds men in the New Covenant is the law of love. If we are to be one with the Godhead, we must be one in love with one another (Mt 6:12, 18:22, 19:35; Lk 17:4). It is this law of love which Christ leaves to his Church to apply "in each particular case or for every age and every local condition".[11] And it is important, for our purposes, to note one of the first such interpretations, that by St. Paul, with regard to the banquet of unity, the Christian eucharist, in chastizing those who come to the eucharist as violators of the law of love (specifically concerning the *agape* feast which was being abused by factionism).[12] The Body must exclude from its greatest moment of unity, the eucharist, those who militate against the very unity of the body. It

10. Cf. **Transformation in Christ**, chap. 6.
11. **The Theology of Sin**, p. 28.
12. Cf. I Cor 12:28-29 and chap. 1, supra.

must also exclude those who threaten its very life, such as heretics (I Tim 1:20; II Tim 2:17; I Jn 2:18; II Jn 10; I Tim 5:11), and also those who commit heinous violations of Christian moral law (I Cor 5:1; Eph 4:1-5:20). This is because, as Paul notes, "If one member suffers, all suffer together" (I Cor 12:26). The health of Christ's body, as in a physical body, can be damaged by a malignant member, which must be excised if the body is to live.

How did the Apostolic Church deal with the possibility that one who chose to embrace the Christian message and its obligations might later fail in carrying out all of its implications, and then repent of the failure? It is difficult to say, A. M. Henry notes, how the institution of Penance functioned in the Apostolic communities.[13] "What is clearly evident," he says, "is that Baptism remitted sins (Acts 2:38), but we do not see that remission was assured by a special rite. On the contrary, the extreme severity against the sins of baptized Christians (see Heb 6:4-8, 10:26-31) seems to have excluded recourse to another sacrament by a second forgiveness. This severity was doubtless necessary to manifest the grandeur of the new life brought by Christ."[14] However, the same author tells us, regardless of changes in the penitential practice of the Church over the centuries, ". . . she has always maintained, as she still does today, that she was remitting sins in the name of God through powers received from Christ."[15] And we gain insight into the role of the Church in this regard by noting the meaning of Christ's words in Mt 16:19 and 18:18, when he gives the apostles power to bind and loose on earth and in heaven. Paul F.

13. A. M. Henry and M. Mellet, "Penance", **Christ in His Sacraments**, Vol. VI in A. M. Henry, ed, **Theology Library** (Chicago: Fides, 1958), tr. Angeline Bouchard, p. 206.
14. Ibid., p. 207.
15. Loc. cit.

An Agonizing Reappraisal

Palmer explains the contextual meaning of these terms:

> The metaphor "to bind and to loose" can have three meanings:
> (1) the magical power of casting a spell over a person and then
> releasing him; (2) the legislative power granted a rabbi or teacher
> of declaring what was forbidden (bound) or permitted (loosed) in
> the Mosaic Law; (3) the judicial power of judging an individual and
> imposing a ban of excommunication (to bind) and afterwards of
> restoring or reconciling the excommunicate to the community (to
> loose).
>
> Without denying that the power given to Peter and to the Twelve
> was legislative as well as judicial, the Fathers of the Church will
> stress the strictly judicial power of the bishops to bind by excom-
> municating and to loose by reconciling the sinner to the Church.
> That this reconciliation will affect the sinner's relationship with God
> as well as with the Church is clear from the formula in which the
> power of binding and loosing is promised: "Whatever you bind
> on earth shall be bound in heaven" (Mt 18:18). In other words,
> whom the Church excludes God excludes; whom the Church
> reconciles to herself God reconciles to Himself . . .[16]

Elsewhere Palmer sheds further light on this notion:

> Basic to Jewish-Christian tradition is the belief that man is saved
> in and through the **community**. If he was to live at all, **he had to
> be one with the community, one with the people of God.** To be
> separated from the community was death. To be restored to the
> community was life. The early Christian did not believe that he
> could have access to God apart from the community. (Emphasis
> added.)[17]

In our next considerations, we shall examine the ritual
of the early Church regarding the Sacrament of Penance,
keeping in mind that this ritual is arranged on the basis of
the theological considerations in the New Testament which
we have just surveyed.

16. Paul F. Palmer, **Sacraments and Forgiveness, Sources of Christian
    Theology,** Vol II (Westminster, Md.: Newman Press, © 1958), p. 3.
17. "The Theology of the **Res et Sacramentum** with Particular Emphasis
    on its Application to Penance", in **Proceedings** of the Catholic Theolog-
    ical Society of America (CTSA), 1959, p. 120.

3. *The Practice of the Early Church.*

The ritual of the early Church, which we shall note here, will provide us with significantly more than a survey of rubrical antiquity; our examination of the early penitential ritual, rather, will prove valuable insofar as it reflects the theology of the New Testament and the development of that theology in the tradition of the Church. (Here, then, we should hasten to note that our study cannot be of the *sacramentum "tantum"* of Penance, but that it is promoted by a concern with the very *nature* of the Sacrament of Reconciliation.)

In the period following the Apostolic era, the Church remained severe in considering the serious moral failures of baptized Christians, but showed salutary willingness to utilize the binding and loosing power given by Christ. "When the good shepherd has found the lost sheep," says A.-M. Roguet, "he does not keep it apart from the rest, but puts it back among its brothers in the flock. Jesus had to die in order 'to gather together in one the children of God that were dispersed' (John 11:52). The whole purpose of the Redemption is that and nothing else . . . And so also in the Church, in the early days, public penance was a recognized thing."[18] In considering the third century as important in the history of penance, Henry notes that "The predominant tendency was toward severity . . . in Tertullian *(De pudicitia)*, Hippolytus *(Philosopheumena)*, Origen *(De oratione)*, St. Cyprian *(Testimonia, De lapsis)*. Emphasis seems to have been upon exterior reconciliation with God. But the thesis of severity led the heretics . . . to such excesses that the Doctors (of the Church) reacted by a gradual shift of emphasis to the interior mystery of repentance and for-

18. A.-M. Roguet, **Christ Acts Through Sacraments** (Collegeville, Minn.: The Liturgical Press, 1954), p. 91.

giveness."[19] He later remarks that the "practical notion of Penance as a visible rite exercised by a social authority that re-establishes the normal relations of grace between God and the soul" stems from a reaction against Montanism in the third century,[20] and that public penance prevailed until the sixth century, from which time until 1215 (the date of the fourth Lateran Council) the emphasis evolved towards private penance.[21]

In discussing the public penance that took place, we should first take account of the relationship between Penance and Holy Eucharist, i.e., the necessity of purification before approaching the Lord's banquet table, as seen in the *Didache*: ". . . (14) And on the Lord's own day, come together and break bread, and make a Eucharist. But first, confess your sins, that your sacrifice may be pure."[22] While there were private penances in certain cases (and while Palmer notes the lack of a *Confiteor* in the ancient liturgies),[23] the Western Church knew one essentially similar form for public penance,[24] which we shall undertake to describe briefly. The penitential ritual, as related by Josef A. Jungmann, took place in the public assemblies of the Church, and usually in three stages:[25]

The first stage involved the confession of the penitent's sin to the president of the assembly, viz., the bishop or (especially as time went on) the priest *(parokios)* as the

19. Henry, op. cit., p. 208.
20. Ibid., p. 209.
21. Ibid., p. 211.
22. As quoted in Palmer, **Sacraments and Forgiveness**, p. 12. This might well be considered in comparison with Pedersen, **Israel;** cf. fn. 7, supra.
23. Loc. cit.
24. Josef A. Jungmann, **The Early Liturgy to the Time of Gregory the Great** (Notre Dame, Ind.: University of Notre Dame Press, 1959), tr. F. Brunner, pp. 249ff. Here it is noted that private penance was not unknown, especially in administering the sacrament to the dying.
25. Loc. cit.; also cf. Jungmann's **Public Worship: A Survey,** tr. Clifford Howell (Collegeville, Minn.: The Liturgical Press, 1957), pp. 77ff.

bishop's delegated representative. Public confession of the sin itself was demanded only in cases of grave *public* sins which directly affected the community as a whole; serious *private* sins were to be confessed privately, and then the person's acceptance into the ranks of the penitents and the fixing of the penance completed the first stage.[26] Effort was made to choose penances which would be "medicinal" in character—which would not be mere punishments, but which would help to elicit in the penitent a spirit of repentance for his sin. Jungmann gives this account of the penitential ritual:

> The official acceptance into the ranks of the penitents used to take place in public divine service; in Rome it was just after Mass. The sinners had to come forward and prostrate themselves, whereupon the bishop addressed to them words of warning and imposed his hand upon them, to the accompaniment of prayers. This was the first blessing of the penitents. The type of prayer which the bishop used appears to have been similar to that which still occurs during Lenten Masses in the form of the **oratio super populum.** After it the penitents were given the rough penitential garb . . . and were expelled from the community of the faithful. From that moment they were considered excommunicated; that is, they were held to have cut themselves off by their sins from the community of saints. Sprinkling the penitents with ashes is also an extremely ancient custom; but later it became combined with this first laying on of hands (Ash Wednesday).[27]

The second stage involved the time of penance itself. The length of this time in individual cases was up to the discretion of the bishop. In some cases penances were arduous and lasting for some time (e.g., a married person might be required to abstain from intercourse for all of Lent).

> During the time of their penance the sinners often received the blessing of the bishop—it might be given to them even daily.

26. Cf. Roguet, loc. cit.: "Anyone who proposes to do penance for his sins has to apply to the bishop . . ."
27. Jungmann, loc. cit.

> Penitents had to fast, say prayers while kneeling, wear penitential garments, and renounce the care of their bodies (by neither bathing nor cutting the hair), also they had to give up the use of marriage . . . In other places sinners were subjected to a mild type of imprisonment.[28]

The last step in the penitential ritual, that of reconciliation, effected the re-introduction of the penitent into the worshipping community. In gleaning accounts from the Gelasian Sacramentary, ca. 700, Barton tells us that the rite took place, appropriately, on Holy Thursday, feast of the eucharist, and that it began with the penitent coming forward and prostrating himself, while a request was made in his behalf by the deacon to the bishop, who warned the penitent[29] that the offense which had been removed by penance could not be repeated. Finally, prayers were said, including a form of absolution.[30] After official reconciliation to the assembly by the bishop came the penitent's joyous return to the Eucharist.[31]

(There is a question as to whether the imposition of hands by the bishop formed an important part of the reconciliation ritual. While no rubrics for it appear in the Gelasian Sacramentary, says Palmer, other references, e.g., by St. Innocent I [402-427] and St. Leo the Great [440-461] and in the third century *Didascalia Apostolorum,* indicate its presence, and it is possible that it was common enough a practice so that it did not necessitate a specific rubric in the Gelasian Sacramentary.[32])

In short, the penitential rite of the early Church indeed strikes a marked contrast between the state of sin and that

28. Ibid., pp. 78-79.
29. Again, this could be done by a priest (**parokios**) representing the bishop.
30. John Barton, **Penance and Absolution** (London: Burns & Oates, 1961), pp. 72ff.
31. Jungmann, loc. cit.
32. Palmer, **Sacraments and Forgiveness**, pp. 113, 118, 63.

of grace, rejecting from the Body of Christ those members who had threatened that body's health, then providing for the healing of those sick members, and finally welcoming them back as again functioning, live and healthy members of the body, able to take part again in that body's supreme activity, the eucharistic liturgical celebration. In considering the significance of the reconciliation of penitents in this context, Rondet says:

> . . . Public penance has a strongly marked social character. It begins with a salutary excommunication. The sinner who submits himself to it is invisibly excommunicated by his sin; he lets this separation be publicly revealed. But this self-suppression already marks the beginning of reintegration, this external excommunication is a partial lifting of the interior excommunication. The Church takes charge of this sick member, she binds him only to unbind him one day. As St. Augustine remarks (**Enchiridion**, c., 65; P.L., 40, 262-263), she acts like a doctor who applies a bandage. He only ties it on to cure, and unties it later on. The body heals the wounds of its members. At the same time, he saw that sin affects the Church. The sinner has offended God, otherwise there would be no sin properly speaking, but he has also wounded the Body of Christ. He has introduced a source of infection and of corruption into the Church. If everyone were to do the same, the Body would come to its end through self-corruption. Thus, every sin has a sociological aspect, in the strong sense of the word, and this is true for even greater reason when the sin, due to its nature, its external character, is an offense against the community.[33]

The public ritual for the Sacrament of Penance, or Reconciliation, as we have just surveyed it, made clear the *ecclesial* or communal nature of sin and reconciliation. As can be seen from the above, however, it was extremely rigorous in itself, and in the fact that it was normally allowed to be administered to a given individual only once for grave reason—thus most Christians probably had no reason to

---

33. Rondet, **The Theology of Sin**, pp. 45-46. Also cf. Clifford Howell, "The Health of the Mystical Body", **Orate, Fratres**, XXV (June, 1951), pp. 301-310 and A. Stoltz, "The Sacraments as Medicine", Ibid., XV (April 20, 1941), pp. 241-248.

avail themselves of this sacrament during the early centuries of Church history.[34] Here we must emphasize the fact that this type of penitential ritual was utilized for situations quite different in range from the practical use of Penance in our own era: frequent confession for venial sin was not the rule, as it later tended to become in the lives of countless Catholics. For Penance to become a regular part of the spiritual lives of Catholics in general, of course, it was necessary not only that its scope be widened, but also that its severity be lessened. That is just what took place in the next stage of development. As Henry describes it:

> . . . discipline gradually gave way to ideas of mercy, as the spiritual effects of penance, i.e., the sacramental character of the penitential rite—were more clearly understood. When the sinner had been liberated from his sins by the Church, he was liberated before God. But at the same time that the idea of penance became more interior and the drama of conscience took precedence over the sentiment of guilt, there was a trend away from public penance toward private penance . . ."[35]

That last development, the widespread gravitation toward private penance, would be an especially important one in the lessening of earlier severities, and in paving the way for the popular use of the Sacrament of Reconciliation not only for the forgiveness of heinous offenses against the moral demands of the Gospel, but for the routine ascetical and moral practices of Christians seeking not only goodness but perfection. More and more, this would become emphasized in what eventually became the custom of the recent past.

4. *The Present Ritual.*
Elsewhere in this volume, we have made note of the

---

34. Indeed, St. Augustine probably never went to Confession, suggests Garry Wills, **Bare Ruined Choirs**, p. 31.
35. Henry, op. cit., p. 211. Concerning the trend toward private penance replacing public penitential ceremonies, cf. ibid., p. 210.

ways in which the conduct of the liturgy in the Roman Rite has been heavily influenced by monasticism.[36] While this has surely been the case with regard to the "liturgical movement" in the later nineteenth and early twentieth centuries, it is no less the case with regard to the matter at hand, i.e., popular Catholic practice concerning the Sacrament of Penance. For centuries of Western Catholic history, we now realize, it has been at least difficult for a distinct lay spirituality—or even a distinct secular spirituality[37]—to develop and function, owing to the predominance of monastic models. This means that the spiritual practices of the Catholic laity have tended to be watered-down emulations of monastic practice.[38] Hence, the tendency of monastics to confess as regularly as once a week tended to be imitated by the laity, at least those who desired to be, or to be considered, good and devout Catholics. The imitation was not always exact, e.g., confession for the layman might have taken place monthly or twice a month rather than weekly. But the underlying motive was the same: striving for Christian perfection. The truly devout Catholic was not likely to be the penitent of antiquity, who had publicly affronted the Christian community by his grave sin of larceny, adultery, murder or the like. He was apt to be a *good* person who wanted to be a *better* person, to improve on this or that tendency or habit, to rectify a certain weakness or imperfection. For such persons, the notion of regular Penance as preventive medicine and moral-and-spiritual tonic became quite popular.[39]

Now, in the wake of the Second Vatican Council (though

36. Cf. Chapters 2, 3, 4, supra.
37. In this context I include those clergy who technically are "secular" but who in lifestyle and spirituality have become heavily monastic.
38. This was the case, too, in the liturgical fashions that prevailed just prior to the Second Vatican Council. Cf. Wills, op. cit., pp. 38-60.
39. Cf. Mayer, art. cit., and **Transformation in Christ**, loc. cit. Most devotional literature up until about 1965 bears out this notion.

by no means simply as a *result* of the Council[40]), it has become more the trend to *de*-emphasize Confession as a regular practice for at least the average lay Catholic, and perhaps even for religious and clerics as well. Furthermore, in many places it was recently the practice to discourage Confession for children before First Communion, and this has brought about no small degree of controversy within the Catholic community.[41] And these problems still leave the question of our coming to grips with sin and reconciliation as communal or *ecclesial*, rather than individual, realities. All of this makes for much consternation among pastors, liturgists and laymen alike.[42]

I should like to make several observations concerning the present ritual, both in its utilization in the very recent past and present, and also with reference to what directions might be taken in future.

First of all, it should be clear at the outset that we are bound neither to continue the practice of the recent past in the name of "tradition" (since the recent past so often is not genuinely "traditional"),[43] nor to ape some era of antiquity out of the conviction that only in this way can we faithfully preserve the faith and practice of Christianity

---

40. Cf. my observations on what I consider the exaggerated significance of Vatican II in my book **American Catholicism** (Englewood Cliffs, N.J.: Prentice-Hall, Inc., 1975), Chapter 1.

41. Cf. Francis J. Buckley, **I Confess** (Notre Dame, Ind.: Ave Maria Press, 1972), for a lucid treatment of some of these issues, and also **Transformation in Christ**, loc., cit.

42. Msgr. George A. Kelly, in an article on this subject, expresses the questions from the point of view of a "typical" Catholic layman; this seems significant in light of the fact that the laity are concerned about questions pertinent to Confession and the moral order in a way quite similar to that depicted by Msgr. Kelly's narrative: George A. Kelly, "Why Not Confession before First Communion?" (New York: unpublished MS, 1972).

43. Cf. Charles Kohli, "A Time to Be at One", in **To Be A Man**, p. 141, and **Transformation in Christ**, p. 61.

as entrusted to the Apostles.[44] We must acknowledge the fact that our carrying out of the apostolic mandates, and our enactment of the sacramental rituals, will admit of adaptation to various times, cultures and circumstances, and that we will often be unable to label one or another as "the right way" *semper et ubique*.[45]

The next thing that is in order, I believe, is to recognize the distinction between that which is essential to the conduct of the Sacrament of Penance and its necessary function in the lives of Christians, viz., forgiveness of grave sin,[46] and that which is not essential but may be salutary or at least desirable, e.g., frequent confession of minor offenses and imperfections. In this regard we will likely find that frequent confession need no longer be insisted upon, but neither should "devotional confession" as a spiritual practice be expunged from Catholic life. Thus, in the long run, our use of the Sacrament of Reconciliation will likely become less regular, and probably less mechanical, less rushed, more helpful. Even if we no longer consider frequent confession to be so rigidly expected as in the past, I suggest in *Transformation in Christ*, "We will have recourse to it often enough, I think, when we realize our own inadequacy in our efforts to fulfill ourselves as Christians . . ."[47] Along the same lines, I think the Catholic community will become increasingly aware that confession before receiving the eucharist is unnecessary except in the presence of grave sin, and hence normally unnecessary for children about to receive Holy Communion for the first time, and for the first

44. Pius XII warned against this type of antiquarianism in the liturgical renewal in his encyclical on the Sacred Liturgy **Mediator Dei,** AAS XXXIX (1947): 521-95.
45. Cf. John Henry Newman, **An Essay on the Development of Christian Doctrine** (London: Longmans, Green & Co., 1897).
46. Cf. fn. 1, supra.
47. **Transformation in Christ,** p. 132.

many times—at least—in their young lives. At the same time, though, I am sure we should avoid the extreme of some pastors or religious educators who positively forbid confession before First Communion for children.[48]

5. *Celebrating the Sacrament of Reconciliation today.*

The type of consideration we have just given to the historical development of the Sacrament of Penance should be helpful to us in arriving at ways of dealing with some of the dilemmas Catholics face today concerning the meaning and use of the Sacrament. And it appears that a certain flexibility will be the order of the day in this regard. But we must yet strike home concerning the central point, as I see it: sin and reconciliation as communal or *ecclesial* realities. At least until very recently, we have tended to view Catholic moral obligations in a narrow perspective, as applying solely to one's own personal moral conduct (and I am told by Protestant friends that they have experienced the same problem in their own denominations as well): personal devotions, fulfillment of Mass obligations, fast regulations, the guidelines offered by the Ten Commandments (stealing, adultery, lying being avoided; honor being given to God and to proper authorities in the world), all too often seemed to suffice for a moral posture which was essentially *defensive*. Walk down the road to salvation, we so often seemed to think, without being harmed by any of the dangers along the way, never veering to the sidelines or getting tangled in the vines overhead; being so careful as to never fall into the

---

48. The discipline of the Church, as expressed early in 1973, was said to call upon American dioceses and parishes to halt "experimental" allowance of children receiving communion before confessing, but it appears, as F. Buckley suggests, that the Roman decree only prohibits banning confession before first communion for those who wish it; canonical evidence supports his interpretation, as do I.

[175]

7

occasional traps that would be in our path. But, of course, a defensive and isolationistic moral posture or policy would necessarily be insufficient for a life of Christian witness. And while we make a gross error if we ignore personal moral obligations (as some have tended to do of late), we must insist that morality consists of more than these. Roguet says it well:

> Our approach to the sacrament of Penance will be quite different if we look upon it from the point of view of our life in the community. Too many Catholics, always ready to make allowances in their own favour, find that they have committed hardly any sins. This is because they restricted their examination of conscience to the commandments of God and the Church which they might have transgressed formally. Since they have not committed murder or theft they can find only simply material little sins, not too humiliating, such as . . . being late for Sunday Mass. Realize your solidarity with your neighbor, and remember that the first, if not the only, commandment is that of fraternal charity; that you are not only required to work out your own salvation but that you are also responsible in the eyes of God for . . . your fellow Christians and the advancement of the kingdom of God. Now you will find something to confess . . ."[49]

If it is for the good health of the entire Body of Christ that each individual member of the Church realize the *ecclesial* dimensions of sin and reconciliation, then we must seek ways in which this realization can be engendered. While many educative efforts in the Church can be helpful, none will be quite so telling as the actual liturgical conduct of the Sacrament of Reconciliation itself for determining future attitudes toward Penance among Catholics.[50] How can this best be done within the context of the present ritual?

First of all, we must remember some of the liturgical principles considered earlier in this book, i.e., a certain economy with regard to change, and a certain flexibility

49. Roguet, op. cit., p. 94.
50. Cf. Donald McDonald, "Essays in Our Day", in **The Catholic Herald-Citizen** (Milwaukee, Wis.), January 3, 1964.

with regard to implementation and adaptation of certain liturgical procedures. This would imply that in dealing with the Sacrament of Penance, it would be well to keep external alterations to a certain minimum, or to introduce them against a background of abiding stability in the Catholic religious experience.[51]

My own suggestions in this regard would call for taking maximum advantage of existing liturgical practices in most American Catholic parishes.[52] In this regard, confessions would continue to be auricular, would continue to be offered on a regular schedule on Saturdays and eves of holy days of obligation, and would continue to afford convenience, frequency and anonymity to those many Catholics who would in all probability desire those factors to continue to be avaliable. Eventually the Church might allow Penance to be positioned as a sort of preface to the Saturday vigil Masses, which anticipate the Sunday celebration. Thus the liturgical reconciliation could culminate in the celebration of the eucharist, as in the penitential rituals of old, and the reconciliation of the individual sinner would truly be seen as an occasion for communal rejoicing. In this way, the communal dimensions of sin, moral obligation and reconciliation would be underscored.

A possible way of doing this would be to make the Saturday or vigil Mass of anticipation one which is preceded by confessions, but in which the absolution pertaining to the individual confessions is withheld until the penitential rite of the Mass itself. One argument against this, of course, is that it could serve to confuse the nature of the penitential rite in the Mass. (Perhaps this is why the Church presently does not allow it.)

Another way would be to begin confessions with a brief

51. Cf. Chapter 4, supra.
52. Lex orandi, lex credendi.

Service of the Word, involving perhaps one or two short readings from the Scriptures, and a condensed homily, pertaining to one theme or another involving communal moral responsibility. In time, the Church might allow this to suffice for the Service of the Word that would belong to the particular Mass for that day. So, the Mass itself would begin with the Offertory. Even prior to such a stage of development, the important thing would be to somehow prepare the penitents for the communal dimensions of the Sacrament in which they are to participate, all the while allowing them to continue participating in a way which is individual and private. One might fear here that the old "mechanical" fashion of confession would remain, but it should be remembered that Catholic attendance at the confessional has declined markedly, and the sheer quantity of penitents that approach confessors in the past is simply lower today. Thus the eradication of the old argument that confessions have to be expedited rapidly—even hurriedly—so as to service all the penitents. Also, one would expect that a confessor who would participate in a ritual like the above would be sensitive to the need for a meaningful execution of it. Finally, most confessors today would likely agree that the penitents of today present more complex moral problems than those of yesterday, on the whole, requiring more careful individual assistance. All these signs indicate that meaningful and helpful individual confessions could take place within the context of a liturgical celebration of Penance which emphasizes the Sacrament's *ecclesial* dimensions as well.

Even if it is not desired or feasible to have a Service of the Word before confession, the Service of the Word in the Saturday or vigil Mass, at least, could expand its scope to include some moral instruction related to the themes of sin and reconciliation as communal realities. But whether this type of instruction takes place before confession, after it, or both, the thing to remember is that what is sought is the gradual education of the average penitent so that he becomes concerned with not only his personal morality and spiritual life, but with an apostolic view of moral obligation, and a communal sense of the health or illness of the Body of Christ which is the Church. I use the word *gradual* here with special care, for it seems that we have already done and seen enough damage, in the past decade or so, owing to a desire to "shake 'em up!" This sort of thing typically involves berating a congregation for their hypocrisy and shallowness, then listing a series of dramatic gestures designed to purify them of all their shortcomings in the social arena (gestures which the preacher will often enough articulate without himself implementing!). We have had a surfeit of that and need no more. What we *do* need is to lead Christian communities, in a way which is less dazzling than lasting, to a profound awareness of sin and grace as communal realities, in light of the individual Christian's membership in the Body of Christ, the Church. If this can be achieved, the individual Christian's life and membership in the Church will mean all the more.[53]

---

53. These considerations are not for those who do not need them, viz., specific worshipping communities that may well have already solved any questions pertinent to the communal celebration of Penance. Hence a somewhat "traditionally" or "conservatively" oriented congregation is envisioned here. However, I have recorded my opinions on such questions as individual confession v. general absolution, etc., in **Transformation in Christ**, Chapter 6.

CHAPTER EIGHT

Renewal in the Marriage Liturgy

LET IT BE clear from the outset that what we are dealing with here is a Roman Catholic marriage liturgy. This does not even suggest that we mean to ignore the ecumenical dimensions of marriage as it is coming to be celebrated in our time, but we cannot at this writing develop a detailed response to all of the exigencies that would be introduced by considering those numerous possibilities. For now, suffice it to say that almost every marriage celebrated in some type of ecumenical context will be an incarnation of a very special relationship between two believers and their two somewhat different perceptions and implementations of the worship of the Lord Jesus in the sacramental mystery we call "his Church". Added to this rather unique situation as it will obtain in individual circumstances, there will come into play the general guidelines for ecumenical services that prevail in a particular nation or diocese, and furthermore the interpretation or implementation of those by the immediate authority in question, usually in some connection with the wishes of the persons to be married themselves. In this chapter, we dare not presume to know of all this in advance and to therefore digest and rehearse it succinctly. It will be the case, too, that parties to any sort of interfaith marriage will necessarily have gone through some personal re-examination of their own commitments to each other, their communities of faith and practice, and the Lord himself, asking themselves just what is the meaning of their commitment to Christ in terms that are identified as Lutheran or Roman Catholic or Methodist or Baptist. For

[180]

these, there has often taken place the sort of theological *examen* (however rudimentary) that would be a salutary thing for all Christians.

But we are concerned here with what would be considered a "normal" or "typical" marriage celebration involving two persons who, at least in terms of their religious initiation and upbringing, are Roman Catholics. And it is our hope that anyone to enter into and celebrate Christian marriage in these terms will not simply accept uncritically a whole package of folkways and customs and attitudes that have been passed on to them by the subculture in which they live, and which may in many a case serve not to illustrate but to obfuscate some very important religious values involved in Christian marriage as sacrament.

All of the sacraments are social realities in the context of the Church as Body of Christ.[1] Yet none of the sacraments is so prone to interpretation as personal event in the "private" or individual sense as marriage, owing to the intimacy of the relationship between two human beings towards which marriage as a sacrament and as a social institution is directed. However, this latter factor can sometimes obscure the *ecclesial* dimensions, viz., the implications for the Christian community as a whole, in the celebration of Christian marriage.

From a variety of standpoints, Christian marriage—at least as it is celebrated or understood by the Roman Catholic tradition—*is* an ecclesial ramification of the saving love of Jesus present in the members of his Body the Church both individually and corporately. If understood, this will have significant implications psychologically, intellectually, emotionally and morally as regards the sacrament of marriage in

---

1. Cf. Ep 4:1-5:20 and especially 5:21-32, also **Transformation in Christ,** chap 7.

the context of the sacramental life of the entire Christian worshipping community. However, this will never be understood merely by virtue of theological pronouncements, however profound, frequent or well-circulated. Nor is it likely to be understood in the total community of the Church by virtue of the appreciations of only a few *cognoscenti*. If this sacramental reality is to be appreciated by the total Church, this appreciation should be both reflected and furthermore engendered by the liturgical celebration of marriage.

I believe the common experience of Catholics (at least in the United States) points up two difficulties which seem to prevail in our liturgical execution of marriage, thus far. First is an overemphasis (even today) on the legalistic aspect of marriage. Our vocabulary, in this regard, has too long been surfeited with words like *contract, bond, marital rights, impediments* and the like. Considerations like these obviously have their place in the Roman Rota, and locally in diocesan marriage tribunals. Further, they may at times be opportune in rectory parlors. But they should hardly be included in the general catechesis of the Church concerning marriage. However, at least until quite recently, these terms have been popular in college and high school courses on marriage, and many a Pre-Cana group or similar situation. This tends to make people who anticipate marriage unnecessarily suspicious of or cool to the Church, rather than cultivate the classic image of the Church as a mother. Those who hear such language are apt to envision the Church instead as a sort of eccentric uncle who is a canon lawyer with a one-track mind, a killjoy, someone to be avoided at all costs whenever possible. Certainly not someone to be invited voluntarily to the "celebration". Many theologians (not the least of whom have been Böckle and Schillebeeckx) have lamented the fact that Catholic teaching on marriage has been characterized by prohibitions more than by exhortations.[2] Such an accusation is both terribly harsh and—I fear—terribly true. I am by no means suggesting that the Church would do well to take lightly the responsibilities involved in Christian marriage and its implications, in moral teaching or any other sphere. But we must not allow people to continue holding an image of the Church as an impersonal superstructure whose only interest in the sacrament of matrimony lies in collecting stipends, keeping records, and taking every opportunity to remind the new spouses how difficult will be their lot in this vale of tears.

Is this *really* the way the Church appears to many young Catholics? Sadly enough, yes. Not just to people who are libertines, or who have opposed the magisterium from time immemorial, or who are too dumb or lazy to understand theology and canon law. I mean rather sincere average Catholics who wonder why there is so much ecclesiastical fuss about what they might be doing wrong and so little manifestation of ecclesiastical joy about what they might well be doing right. And if this type of image of the Church prevails, it should be little wonder that the nuptial liturgy in church will be a somewhat mechanical and unwelcome legalistic preamble to "the wedding", i.e., the reception after the liturgy.

The type of Church image described above has resulted in too many Catholics "going through the motions" so far as a nuptial liturgy in the Church is concerned, and thus their attitude towards it becomes one of tolerance at best. Part of the incarnation of this attitude is the spirit of shortening and racing the nuptial liturgy, so the "real" wedding can begin. Another part of it is to make the ecclesiastical cere-

2. Cf. Franz Böckle, ed., "Moral Problems and Christian Personalism", Vol. V of **Concilium** (Glen Rock, N.J.: Paulist Press, 1965) and my own remarks in a piece entitled "Liberate All Priests, Not Only Some", in **The National Catholic Reporter**, August 4, 1972.

mony of marriage tolerable to its participants by making it as personally sentimental as possible in terms of the individual spouses (and/or their families and friends). While the liturgical rites of the Church obviously provide flexibilities and options which are quite legitimate, it can hardly be said that we should allow the worship of the entire *communio sanctorum* to degenerate into a mere celebration of human aspiration without an adoration of the divine intervention into human history. However, that is what is happening in far too many cases. It happened in the "old days", liturgically, when marriage celebrations in church were fifth-rate operatic solos by somebody's Aunt Gertrude ("On this Day, O Beautiful Mother", Schubert's *Ave Maria,* Franck's *Panis Angelicus,* and all the other "golden oldies" that had more to do with sentiment than sacrament). It happens still in the "new liturgy" with the themes from *Love Story* and *Doctor Zhivago.* In either idiom, it is a somewhat unconscious ignorance of the sacrament of marriage as *ecclesial,* and I suspect it is partly because the Church has behaved in such wise as to *ask* to be ignored, or to be tolerated to whatever extent necessary.

The second problem, as I see it, is that our liturgical experience in general, even since the reforms heralded by Vatican Council II, has been all too isolationistic as opposed to communal.[3] Even today, it is a rare parish that regularly offers an experience of real community at the eucharist. I suspect that all the blame for this cannot be assigned to the imperfections in our liturgical exhortations and efforts, but some of it must be allocated to the contrary liturgical experience, which has become part and parcel of so many Catholics' lives. Let us acknowledge, then, that marriage will be one of the last places in which a spirit of liturgical community is apt to flourish, first of all because our cele-

3. Cf. Chapters 4-5, supra.

bration of that sacrament seems to have been more isolationistic than most of our other liturgical experiences in the
Church, and secondly because most of the individuals attending a nuptial liturgy are becoming members of that
particular worshipping assembly for the first and last time
in their respective lives (the same is often true with a
funeral liturgy).

Both of the above problems will ultimately call for solutions of a long-range rather than a short-range nature. The
second problem will admit of some solution in the overall
revitalization of our liturgical experience. The first is far
more complex, and calls for a serious maturation of Catholic
thinking and feeling about sex—and myriad indications from
clerical and lay quarters alike show that this will be a long
and painful time in coming. The second of these problems has
been addressed earlier in this volume,[4] and the first is
outside the proper scope of the present work;[5] however, let
us discuss ways in which the ecclesial dimensions of the
sacrament of marriage can be better appreciated within the
Church as a total worshipping community while solutions
to these two basic problems are yet forthcoming.

We will have to cultivate, within a general liturgical
renewal, a keen awareness of the spouses in marriage as
ministers of the sacrament within the context of the Church
in toto. Two concepts are of special import here: *ministers*
and *(within the context) of the Church*. Man and wife in
Christian marriage are ministers, and the validity of their
ministry in this sacrament depends on the validity of the
sign they give to each other (i.e., their freedom to make
a marital commitment, their understanding of what is essen-

4. Ibid.
5. Cf. **Transformation in Christ,** loc. cit., and the writings of various
Catholic commentators in this area e.g., Andrew M. Greeley, Eugene
C. Kennedy, Mary Perkins and John Julian Ryan.

tial to that commitment, etc.) and not on any other minister. While it is the ritual and discipline of the Church that at least one minister witnesses the marriage, it is wholly incorrect to say he "performs" it. The husband and wife are the ministers; they are dependent on a priest or deacon to witness their action, but not to supplant it. This theological truism, taken out of context, could of course encourage a sort of autonomy on the part of spouses. But in context, that is not where it logically leads. For the spouses in marriage are ministers *of the Church*. This will mean that they are in one sense empowered by the Church to effect the sign of matrimony, but it will also mean that they are *responsible* to the Church for the execution of their ministry. In other words, the ministry is a function not of the two individual spouses, but of the Church as a whole, with the two ministers acting in the person of Christ (as with the minister of any of the Church's sacraments). Historically, we have understood this as meaning that the spouses in marriage are obliged to lead lives of exemplary Christian love and moral virtue. True enough. We would also stress their obligation to understand as thoroughly as possible the meanings of the sacrament they bring to each other and to the Church as community. And it is in that latter regard that we need to work. Spouses often undertake marriage with at least some awareness of the meaning of marriage for themselves; what really needs cultivating, in addition to that, is an appreciation of the meaning of their sacramental state *for the Church as total 'worshipping community*. If this is understood, then it can be seen that the husband and wife *as part of their ministerial function* have both the right and the obligation to lead their fellow Christians in the liturgical celebration of the sacrament.

The spouses do not usurp the witness-function of priest or deacon (that is not their ministerial function), nor do they arrogate to themselves those functions which are properly those of the priest celebrating a Nuptial Mass (for those are not their ministerial functions either). But it is part of their proper liturgical function as ministers of the sacrament of marriage to shape and lead, as much as possible, a liturgical celebration of marriage that will make more manifest within the Christian community as a whole the meaning of this sign of love not only between two Christians but within the very mystery of the relationship of love between Christ and his Body the Church.[6]

If a good job of preparation for the sacrament of matrimony is being done, with the above considerations in mind, Catholics entering into the sacrament will be looking forward to a meaningful celebration of it and not merely the prosecution of a formalistic and impersonal exercise to satisfy requirements and social expectations.

To pursue this further, some concrete considerations are in order:

1. *The place for the celebration.*

While it has been the practice, by canon law and tradition, to celebrate the marriage liturgy in the territorial parish of the bride,[7] it would surely appear that this requirement should be applied as flexibly as possible, if not done away with altogether, in modern times. As I have observed previously in this book,[8] the concept of geographical parish does not mean today what it meant to Catholics yesterday. This will be even more true in the case of young Catholics, i.e., those of commonly marriageable age, whose membership in a worshipping community frequently takes shape in someplace other than a territorial parish, e.g., a

6. Ep 5:21-32.
7. CIC, Can. 1097-9.
8. Chapter 4, supra.

university or hospital chapel, a Newman center, a downtown church, or whatever. Often, young people cease to "live at home" when they graduate from high school or college, but their "parish" remains to be construed as the place where their parents live. This may be an automatic convenience, but it is often unrealistic. There seems no compelling reason why a marriage should be celebrated in a parish where one of the parties (usually the bride) happened to grow up, or to which one's parents moved *after* one had grown up, as is so often the case in today's highly mobile society. In many cases, young people getting married will identify together in terms of a worshipping community that is truly their own, and not just an impersonal institution that is convenient to their residences or those of their parents (like a branch of First National City Bank).[9] Present Canon Law often takes care of legitimate concerns in this regard, but lay people often are not so informed.

2. *The Officiant(s) for the celebration.*

While it is correct that the spouses themselves are the ministers of the sacrament, the celebration of marriage li-

9. My wife grew up in St. Helena's Parish in the Bronx, and I in St. Thomas the Apostle Parish in San Francisco. After I left San Francisco to pursue professional opportunities, my parents moved to Holy Cross Parish in San Francisco and as my wife was finishing senior year of high school and was preparing to go away to college her parents moved to St. Anastasia's Parish in Queens (which, although technically in the same City of New York as the Bronx, is in a different see, viz., the Diocese of Brooklyn). One place we considered to be a worshipping community where we "belonged" was Immaculate Conception Chapel at Seton Hall University (in South Orange, N.J., in the Archdiocese of Newark). At that time (1968), it would have been extremely difficult, ecclesiastically, to celebrate our marriage liturgy there. Incidentally, at that time I was canonically a member of St. Paul's Parish in Irvington, N.J. (although I lived in Maplewood) and I imagine my name was read in the banns there, but I wasn't there to hear it, since I typically attended Mass at the University Chapel at Seton Hall. This very narration should serve to illustrate the points I am trying to make.

turgically will involve a priest or deacon as witness in behalf of the Church. As the restoration of the permanent diaconate, and the assignment of seminarians to diaconal functions in parishes, make their impact on Catholic life, it might be supposed that the witness to marriage will be a deacon in an increasing number of situations.[10] I submit, however, that this would be offset to a large extent by the continuing trend towards celebration of matrimony within the context of the Eucharist, viz., Nuptial Mass, in which case a priest (or concelebrating priests) would be involved as celebrant(s) for the Mass, if not also witness(es) to the exchange of nuptial vows.

In any case, let us remember that random assignment or chance assignment of priest(s) or deacon to officiate at a marriage liturgy is at least as damaging to the celebration as is the type of impersonal selection of a place of celebration which we criticize above. All too often a priest who bears little or no relation to any of the involved parties is "assigned to the task" (it might well become the same in the instance of a deacon). The result is often a mechanical ritual. This type of problem has become increasingly evident in this area of a reformed vernacular liturgy with *versus populum* altars: if a celebrant or officiant is obviously involved in the liturgy, his attitude will be contagious; on the other hand, his lack of involvement can be contagious too.

Again, there will be some need here for flexibility, and it is becoming more and more apparent that a college chaplain or a personal or family friend should often be chosen over a local pastor or curate who has no personal relationship with the spouses, in many a case.

10. For some assessments of the impact of the restored diaconate in the Church, cf. Paul Hoffmann's dispatch from Rome in **The New York Times,** December 10, 1972; **The National Catholic Reporter,** December 16, 1972; and my own remarks in **Commonweal,** Vol 97, No. 14 (January 12, 1973): 316-317.

It should be noted, too, that the possible separation of officiant (or witness) and celebrant, plus the option of con-celebration, will provide for the involvement of many clerics, if desired. Thus in a situation where involvement by more than one priest (or deacon) is seen as desirable, it can be effected.

We cannot hope to offer meaningful observations re-garding liturgical officiants without mentioning the new opportunities for lay persons to perform certain ministerial functions in the liturgy. Laymen can act as acolytes (serv-ers), and often a relative or friend of one of the spouses is a more opportune choice for this function than a young boy from the parish who merely exchanges free play-time for a stipend. However, we have for so long succumbed to the erroneous notion that only males of a certain age, i.e., "altar boys", can perform such tasks, that we have ignored the potential involvement of adults, including even mature men, in the celebration of marriage involving persons dear to them.[11] This case is, of course, an old one, and a model for newer and more applicable (perhaps) possibilities for lay ministerial involvement in the liturgy. Laymen can now function as commentator or director of community worship (I far prefer the latter term)[12] as well as lector, and there is much more opportunity for lay *women* as well to occupy these liturgical roles today than at any previous time we are familiar with. Thus there is an opportunity for the friends or relatives of the bride and groom to partake in the cele-bration not only in the society-page sense of "the wedding party", but even more meaningfully in the ministerial func-tions of the liturgical celebration (the one, of course, not

11. If we forcefully emphasize the function of serving Mass as a most honorable one, we may increase adults' willingness to perform this task.
12. Cf. Chapters 3, 4, 5 supra.

necessarily precluding or co-opting the other).[13]

Of course, another position in the liturgical celebration, particularly pertinent to the Mass as such, is participation in the Offertory Procession. If a congregation is small enough (say, less than a hundred), it is often feasible and desirable for each member of the congregation, in turn, to place in the ciborium his host at the Offertory, in procession. However, congregations are seldom so small, and we are still required to deal with the fact that not every congregant is necessarily a communicant. Thus we usually have in our churches a "representative" or "symbolic" Offertory Procession, in which selected members of the congregation represent their fellows in bringing to the sanctuary and to the celebrant the species of bread and wine to be utilized in that Eucharist. It occurs to me that this type of practice is an ideal opportunity for the parents of the spouses, who have given them life and prepared them for their own marriage, to symbolize their special role in this situation by presenting the gifts at the Offertory of the Nuptial Mass. It is also really preferable, in my view, to having the father of the bride "give the bride away", since this latter custom is purely of a society-page nature, involves only one parent, and smacks of a previous era of arranged marriages when the bride was considered a piece of property given from one man to another.[14]

3. *The Liturgy of Marriage itself.*

The suggestions which follow will assume the following: a) the context of Nuptial Mass, from which the portions pertaining to a nuptial liturgy outside of Mass can be

---

13. I personally would feel that if a friend of mine asked me to take a special part in his marriage liturgy, being invited to read the Epistle would be more an honor than being asked to give a toast or wear a tuxedo.
14. Cf. my remarks in **Transformation in Christ**, loc. cit.

taken for use; b) no distinction between "high" and "low" services, since our experience liturgically indicates the obsolescence of such a demarcation and the desirability of at least some sung prayer in most liturgical celebrations, marriage included; c) those traditions pertinent to marriage celebrations which are purely of social, rather than religious, nature, can all be done away with if so desired, and in many instances supplanted by religious practices which are more appropriate (as mentioned in #2, above); however, some or even all of these could be retained if desired.

The Entrance Rite should involve the spouses and the sacramental witness of matrimony, preceded by the other liturgical ministers (concelebrants, acolytes, lectors, etc.) It may also be desirable to include the parents of the spouses (even though they may be involved in an Offertory Procession) and the non-ordained witnesses ("best man" and maid or matron of honor), who may also function in ministerial roles, e.g., lector. (A conventional procession of bridesmaids, if desired, could be incorporated here as well.) An acclamation in song proclaiming the nature of the celebration is surely most desirable here, but we must not forget the practical or logistical difficulties that would logically ensue should we ask a congregation to concentrate on the reading and singing of a hymn when they would normally and understandably be inclined to watch the Entrance Procession. The obvious thing to do here is to select a psalm-and-refrain acclamation in antiphonal form which can be sung simply and without recourse to hymnals, booklets, cards, sheets or other paraphernalia which would annoy and be ignored by the vast majority of the congregation. Thus the congregation could sing their part of the Entrance Song while not forsaking their attention to the procession, and a cantor (or small *schola cantorum*) could sing the verses. My own suggestion here would be Dennis Fitzpatrick's refrain, "May the God of Israel Join You and Be With You", with appropriate verses from Tobias 7:15 and Psalm 127 (128):1-2.[15] If additional verses are desired, they could be selected from Psalm 127 (128). The verses could be sung according to Fitzpatrick's own system of psalmody, or even another which would be compatible with the refrain in question. An alternate suggestion more pertinent to the nature of the Entrance Rite in general would be Psalm 121 (122) in the Gelineau collection.[16]

In the Penitential Rite, while options are available, it might be most desirable in a Nuptial Mass for the *Kyrie* litany and a series of petitions proper to the celebration in question to be combined (e.g., asking that you will bless *N.* and *N.* entering into Christian marriage, so they may reflect the love between you and your Church, we pray: *Christ, have mercy.*)[17]

The service of the Word should embody maximum utilization of the alternatives made available by the Church in terms of selections from the Bible. By this I do not mean that the more traditionally chosen readings should never be chosen, but simply that they should not be *automatically* chosen or "selected by default" (I personally prefer the traditional Epistle selection from Ephesians 5, for example, but this is not without having considered the alternatives). This can be a meaningful involvement for the bridal couple in the planning of their own liturgical celebration of mar-

15. Dennis Fitzpatrick, ed., **The English Liturgy Hymnal** (Chicago, Ill.: Friends of the English Liturgy, 1965), No. 490. Some may question the appropriateness of some of the Old Testament imagery in Ps. 127 (128). For this reason only vv. 1-2 are definitely suggested here, with the others being optional. Of course, this is no more than a suggestion.
16. Joseph Gelineau, **Twenty-four Psalms and a Canticle** (Toledo, Ohio: Gregorian Institute of America, 1955), tr. and comp. by Gregory Murray and Clifford Howell. Cf. Chapter 5, fn. 22, for more detailed bibliographical reference. Again, no more than a suggestion.
17. **Handbook,** pp. 49-56.

riage, and they will have to choose from among a number of passages reflecting different insights into marriage both theologically and also in terms of the sociology of the place and time of composition. (Some, for instance, would consider a particular passage "anti-feminist"—or more properly speaking, not adequately appreciative of woman's role in marriage, and so on.) While responses to the readings in the Service of the Word can be either sung[18] or spoken, my own suggestion here is that a congregation for a marriage liturgy is probably together as a congregation for the first time and cannot digest too many new elements at once, liturgically, and spoken responses would probably be better at this particular point.[19]

If there should be a homily within the Service of the Word, let it be one which pertains in some way to the particular celebration in question, or perhaps as well to some notions concerning changing ideas on marriage today (e.g., greater appreciation of woman's role, etc.).[20] No one about to preach at a marriage liturgy should simply pull a sermon out of a file (or the "traditional exhortation" out of the *Collectio Rituum*)[21] and consider this adequate preparation for a particular service. Furthermore, with reference to the

---

18. E.g., in the manner described above for antiphonal singing.
19. Cf. my general observations along these lines in Chapter 5, supra.
20. The marriage homily, ideally, should pertain not only to the bridal couple but to the total worshipping community present, i.e., not only to those beginning marriage, but to those married quite some time as well, etc., thus emphasizing the ecclesial nature of this sacrament.
21. Walter J. Schmitz, ed., **Collectio Rituum Pro Diocesibus Civitatum Foederatarum Americae Septentrionalis** (Milwaukee: Bruce, 1964), pp. 456fff. It should be noted that this passage is often printed in pew booklets provided at Nuptial Masses, and read by the worshippers silently as it is read aloud by the celebrant. Furthermore, many lay Catholics who have attended numerous weddings have almost memorized the material as well as the people who recite it (including those who attempt to make it appear original in their delivery). Thus omitting a reading of it at the nuptial liturgy hardly obliterates it.

"traditional exhortation", it should be stressed here that I strongly oppose its continued use for the following reasons: First, even among celebrants/officiants who select and read it with the greatest of sincere fervor, this traditional passage has by now become associated with something taken out of a file (as I noted before). Or, what is perhaps worse, many Catholics have come to consider it a part of the official liturgy of marriage, which it is not. Secondly, and more importantly, the theological expressions implied in the "traditional exhortation" are woefully lopsided, in their overemphasis on the spouses' obligations to procreate (which they will likely do anyway) and on the numerous pitfalls which seem necessary to balance any happiness they may experience in the marital state. The exhortation reflects a mindset which is somewhat Jansenistic in its implications that marriage is somehow a sort of second-class Catholic life, tolerable only because it may result in fruitful issue. This sort of thing, in my own opinion, is insulting to the intelligence, integrity and maturity of the spouses entering into marriage, and helps to create some of the very atmosphere which I lamented earlier in this chapter, resulting in many Catholics' lack of genuine trust of and love for the institutional Church as they approach the day of marriage.

It might be asked here, "Should the prospective spouses be given moral training *at all* in preparation for marriage, then?" Of course! But the day of the marriage liturgy is by no means an opportune time to provide "last-minute" instructions that should be part of a lifelong preparation in the home and the total community of the believing Church. And if that lifelong preparation has been wanting, the chances of its lacunae being filled by a brief instruction during the marriage liturgy are pathetically slight.

In the Offertory Rite of Nuptial Mass, as we have suggested before, a particularly apt ceremony would be the presenting of the gifts for the eucharistic celebration by the parents of the spouses (or by other appropriate parties in the instance of deceased parents). Again, the congregation will be attending to a procession, and it is probably un-realistic to attempt to engage them in singing anything beyond a simple refrain at this time. An offertory hymn could be sung by a choir (often, this is a good spot for an appro-priate "folk hymn") in lieu of congregational sung prayer at this point. Here I must insist, however, that whatever be sung be in some way representative of the entire congrega-tion, whether it be singing by the congregation *in toto,* by the congregation in alternation with a cantor/leader of song, or by a choir or *schola* representing the total worshipping community. However, this end is not achieved by a solo performance of some sentimental favorite, whether that be "Old Chestnut" or whatever may be its contemporary equivalent. (This norm should prevail in all parts of all liturgical celebrations, not just here.)

The Communion Rite of the Nuptial Mass should in-volve the total worshipping community, as in any celebration of the Mass. Until recently, it had been commonly believed by Catholics that receiving communion at a Nuptial Mass, or a funeral mass for that matter, constituted some kind of breach of Catholic etiquette, in that this Mass supposedly belonged not to the Catholic community as a whole, but to the person(s) for whom it was being offered (in marriage, for the spouses; in death, for the deceased). We are now making strides in replacing such false propriety with notions which enjoy greater theological propriety, to the effect that every eucharistic celebration involves the whole Church, and that every member of that Church present therefore should endeavor to partake in communion. There are ways in which we can contribute to this maturation in Catholic eucharistic piety, even beyond the general efforts of the Church which have borne such fruit over the last seventy or so years. First, by our general style of celebrating the Nuptial Mass, we can make clear that it is a community celebration, not just a nice Currier and Ives portrait to be viewed with sentimental awe. This is achieved by just such elements as congregational participation in sung prayer when appropriate, the careful choice of Biblical readings, the formation and execution of a homily, a parental offertory procession, and the like. It can also be achieved by setting a tone for the Nuptial Mass before it even takes place, with particular regard to communion. One way of doing this is phrasing a wedding invitation in such wise as to make clear the nature of the celebration. Some wedding invitations of late have included a footnote inviting congregants to "receive Holy Communion with the bridal party". This, however, implies that the invitation is special or exceptional, and that the prerogative of inviting to the eucharistic banquet belongs not to the Lord but to the bridal party. I much prefer wording which both explains and presumes the nature of the celebration, e.g., "You are invited to join in the Eucharistic Celebration where N. and N. will join themselves . . ."[22]

Of course, the communal nature of the celebration, particularly at communion time itself, can also be brought out by an appropriate musical selection by a choir or *schola*, or preferably by the congregation alternating with a cantor or *schola*. (Some of the entrance hymns suggested above would fit here, as would Fitzpatrick's *Ubi Caritas* or Jabusch's *Whatsoever You Do*.)[23] Of course, other antiphonal

22. This wording is, of course, only a suggestion. The reader will note that I have also contrived to stress the fact that the spouses join themselves in marriage, which is the most theologically accurate way of describing their ministerial roles in this case. I have not mentioned the parents of the bride as "sponsoring" or inviting people to the wedding because it really isn't theirs, and perpetuating the supposition that it is seems only to perpetuate a host of questionable stereotypes. Their inclusion in the sort of wording I propose is possible if desired, however.
23. Cf. Fitzpatrick, op. cit., No. 990. Jabusch's hymn is published fre-

selections could be used here,[24] as could a number of "folk hymns", such as Rivers' *God Is Love,*[25] or Scholtes' *They'll Know We Are Christians by Our Love,*[26] to mention just a couple of the more popular examples of this category.

The period for meditation after communion provides an ample opportunity for an appropriate musical selection by a choir or *schola,* or instrumentally, either in a "folk" liturgical idiom or of a more traditional style.[27] Finally, the liturgy can conclude with a joyous recssional which embodies the witness of the whole Christian community to the celebration of the marriage of two Christians.[28] Then a reception can take place which is truly an outgrowth of the liturgical celebration, and which is less likely to be disproportionate in style and expense to a mechanical ecclesiastical preamble.[29] In such a way, by truly celebrating marriage as a

quently in the **Monthly Missalette** of the J.S. Paluch company in Chicago, used in a great number of American Catholic parishes.

24. E.g., Fitzpatrick, op. cit., Nos. 521, 780, 994, 999, 1024, 1246-1250.
25. Published originally in Clarence Rivers' **An American Mass Program** (Cincinnati: World Library of Sacred Music, 1964) and since then in subsequent releases by the same publisher.
26. From the **Hymnal for Young Chistians** (Chicago: F.E.L., 1966). Of course, the hymnal contains other good selections, and some of the more popular ones, of which Scholtes' hymn is one, are published elsewhere and in subsequent editions. F.E.L. is the abbreviated title which began to be used in 1965 and thereafter by Dennis Fitzpatrick's Friends of the English Liturgy. For an explanation of this intriguing nomenclature, cf. **Transformation in Christ,** Chapter 1, fn. 3.
27. Most couples planning a marriage ceremony would likely have in mind a number of selections in this regard. They should keep in mind the appropriateness of any particular selection to the liturgy and the congregation as a whole, and not just themselves, as well as the possibility of any given selection being performed adequately in terms of existing resources (singers, instruments, players).
28. Possibilities abound here. One of my favorites is **Give Them, O Lord** (Full Length of Days), in Fitzpatrick, op. cit., No. 849; it can be sung to the familiar "Old Hundredth" melody.
29. The anxiety which immigrant and second-generation Catholics have about proclaiming their arrival in the New World of "WASP America" can be seen in the lavish—indeed downright outlandish—wedding receptions that are usually in evidence on the East Coast. Midwestern and

sign of love and grace in the community of the Church, we underscore in Catholic community life the communal dimensions of marriage—and the importance of the Church in each marriage involving her members—in a manner far more profound than could be achieved by innumerable exhortations, instructions, encyclicals and the like. *Lex orandi, lex credendi.*[30]

West Coast Catholics are farther in time and distance from the "old country", more Americanized, and more apt to have a less elegant and exorbitant celebration.

30. Literally, the law of praying is the law of believing. Or put into context, liturgical worship-expressions reflect and influence the belief of the community more profoundly—in many cases—than the official pronouncements of the community in question.